WORD OF LIFE

**ADVENT EDITION
SEPTEMBER–DECEMBER 1991**

HODDER AND STOUGHTON
and
THE SALVATION ARMY

British Library Cataloguing in Publication Data
  Words of life. September–December 1991
    1. Christian life – Daily readings
    242'.2

  ISBN 0-340-55358-8

Copyright © 1991 by The Salvation Army. First published in Great Britain 1991. All rights reserved. No part of this publication may be reproduced or transmitted in any form or by any means, electronic or mechanical, including photocopying, recording, or any information storage or retrieval system, without either prior permission in writing from the publisher or a licence permitting restricted copying. In the United Kingdom such licences are issued by the Copyright Licensing Agency, 90 Tottenham Court Road, London W1P 9HE. The right of The Salvation Army to be identified as the author of this work has been asserted by them in accordance with the Copyright, Designs and Patents Acts 1988.

Published by Hodder and Stoughton, a division of Hodder and Stoughton Ltd, Mill Road, Dunton Green, Sevenoaks, Kent TN13 2YA. Editorial Office: 47 Bedford Square, London WC1B 3DP.

*Photoset by Rowland Phototypesetting Ltd
Bury St Edmunds, Suffolk
Printed in Great Britain by Clays Ltd, St Ives plc*

CONTENTS

'Spiritual Discernment'

With the Man, Jesus
(Mark Chapters 1–8)
1 September–2 October

With a Remarkable Visionary
(The Prophecies of Ezekiel)
3–24 October

With an Impetuous Follower
(The First Letter of Peter)
25 October–12 November

With a Practical Prophet
(Zechariah Chapters 1–8)
13–30 November

Within the Early Church
(Acts Chapters 1–5)
2–31 December

Advent Readings
(Selected Passages)
(1, 8, 15, 22–26 December)
Comments by Major Ron Thomlinson

ABBREVIATIONS USED FOR BIBLE VERSIONS

KJV   Authorised (King James) Version
NKJV   New King James' Version
GNB   Good News Bible
JB   Jerusalem Bible
JBP   J. B. Phillips – The New Testament in Modern English, 1972 edition
LB   The Living Bible – Kenneth Taylor
NEB   The New English Bible
REB   The Revised English Bible
NIV   New International Version
RSV   Revised Standard Version
WB   William Barclay's Translation

Although numbers of different versions are quoted in *Words of Life* any one of the above versions is adequate for study purposes, though remember, if you use the *KJV* that many of the meanings of words have changed over the centuries. For some readers the *Revised Authorised* version may prove helpful, even though it is not quoted in this volume.

Other Abbreviations:

SASB   The Song Book of The Salvation Army, 1986
HFTC   Hymns for Today's Church, Hodder & Stoughton, 1982
WoL   Words of Life

SUNDAY 1 SEPTEMBER
GOOD NEWS

READING MARK 1:1–3
'The beginning of the gospel about Jesus Christ, the Son of God . . . Prepare the way for the Lord, make straight paths for him' (vv. 1,3b, NIV).

THE GOSPEL BEGINS WITH PREPARATION. More than two thousand years of Hebrew history were required before people were ready to hear. Abraham and the Patriarchs; Moses, Joshua and the Judges; Saul, David, Solomon and a succession of kings; Elijah, Amos, Hosea and many prophets; Ezra and thousands of scribes – these and a multitude of other ordinary and extraordinary people were necessary before Jesus could burst upon the scene with his message of the love and sacrifice of God himself, embodied in his life and ministry. Without those two thousand years of history, Jesus' message would not have been understood.

Mark feels no need to describe the circumstances of Jesus' birth or early childhood. For Mark the good news begins with Jesus, already adult, responding to John the Baptist's message. There is no argument. Mark presents Jesus simply as the Son of God. The historical preparation has all been made. All that is now needed is to prepare individual hearts and minds to receive the gospel. That requires a change of attitude, in other words, repentance.

In one way the situation is still the same today as when John began to preach. The way of the Lord still needs preparation. Anyone who wishes to understand and take hold of the good news of Jesus still has to change their attitude. Our own selfish values have to be turned on their head if the gospel is to have meaning for us, and have meaning for those around us. If we cling to our old ways, the gospel cannot spread. The gospel requires us to be continually renewed, and provides the power for that renewal day by day.

PRAYER SUBJECT: *That the gospel message may spread.*

PRAYER: *Father God, we pray for ourselves, and for all the other people who are spreading the good news of the gospel. May our witness be effective. Help us to reflect our knowledge of the good news in practical, Christian living. Keep us continually aware of the need for renewal in our spiritual life.*

MONDAY 2 SEPTEMBER
JOHN THE BAPTIST

READING MARK 1:4–8
'I baptise you with water, but he will baptise you with the Holy Spirit' v. 8, NIV).

JOHN PREPARED THE WAY for Jesus. Preparation has a value all its own. Abraham, Moses and others we mentioned yesterday were all part of God's preparation, getting men ready to hear the message of Jesus when he came. Each had their own mission to fulfil, quite apart from the fact that they were preparing for the coming of another who would point men directly to God. Indeed, by and large, these Old Testament figures were unaware that their ministry was one of preparation. They were aware of the value of their ministry for their own generation. Some of them knew it would be important for the future, but not that its greatest importance was to prepare for the coming of another.

John was different. He was acutely aware that his mission was to fulfil a ministry of preparation. John's symbolic baptism in water would be replaced by the reality of baptism with the Holy Spirit. How much harder it is to take on a ministry which we know is simply to prepare for the coming of another. How hard it is to perform our task faithfully, knowing that the credit will go to another. John himself found it hard, as his later questioning shows.

Luke 7:19ff.

It is still the calling of all Christian ministers, *(properly understood, minister means every lay person as well as clergy)* to perform our task faithfully, knowing that our faltering efforts are simply preparation for the real work, the work of the Holy Spirit. We may talk, serve, preach, teach, and even baptise, but it is all simply preparation: valuable preparation, but only preparation for the effective work of the Holy Spirit.

TO PONDER *Our task is to prepare the way for Jesus, but it is Jesus himself, through the Holy Spirit, who works in the hearts of men.*

TUESDAY 3 SEPTEMBER
HOLY SPIRIT

READING MARK 1:9–13
'As Jesus was coming up out of the water, he saw heaven being torn open and the Spirit descending on him like a dove' (v. 10, NIV).

THE SPIRIT descended on Jesus at his baptism. It is a beautiful picture, the dove, symbol of peace, alighting on Jesus. It is a gentle picture, in strong contrast to the severe message of John. Yet it is a picture which somehow lacks the dramatic force of some of the other events in Jesus' life. The anguish of the temptations, the pain of rejection in Nazareth, the despair that his disciples will ever understand, the trauma of Gethsemane, the torture of the cross, the glory of the resurrection. All these pictures seem to imprint themselves on our mind with greater clarity than this gentle descent of the dove.

Luke 3:7

Matt 4:1ff.
Luke 4:1ff.
Luke 4:28–30
Mark 4:40
8:21 etc.

We cannot deny that life is full of trauma. But life is also full of gentleness and peace. The dramatic hurly-burly of mission began for Jesus with the gentle picture of the dove descending, bringing calm and order, bringing strength and inspiration to face the trials of the next three years of hectic preaching, teaching and healing.

Acts describes the Holy Spirit coming with tongues of fire. But he also comes, gentle as the dove.

> *He came in semblance of a dove,*
> *With sheltering wings outspread,*
> *The holy balm of peace and love*
>   *On each to shed.*

A VERSE

> *And his that gentle voice we hear,*
> *Soft as the breath of even,*
> *That checks each fault, that calms each fear,*
>   *And speaks of Heaven.*
>   *(Harriette Auber, SASB 200)*

WEDNESDAY 4 SEPTEMBER
FISHERS OF MEN

READING MARK 1:14–20
'Simon and his brother Andrew . . . were fishermen. "Come, follow me," Jesus said, "and I will make you fishers of men"' (vv. 16b, 17, NIV).

FISHERMEN ARE FAMOUS for dedication. With a line, they may stay all day, catching almost nothing. With nets, in boats, they will brave enormous seas to bring their catch home. It is a way of life which demands cutting oneself off from others, and concentrating on fish to the exclusion of everything else.

So, too, with fishers of men. They need dedication to their task. Concentration on the matter in hand is vital. But that concentration is on people, listening to what motivates them, taking notice of their needs, coming alongside them in their everyday experience. That's what evangelism is about.

The fisherman needs to know the habits of the fish. He needs to be able to think himself into their position and try to understand how they will react. With fish that is not too easy. They live in water. However much we learn about them, we can never identify fully with them.

With people it is different. We are all people. We know how people feel and suffer. We know how they react, for we react in similar ways ourselves – or do we? Education and training, intellectual stimulus and even religious development may combine to give some of us a false veneer. Our basic human reactions are covered up to an extent where we no longer know how others feel and think. Discovering in ourselves what is real and what is false, stripping away that veneer of 'hypocrisy', laying ourselves open to God, is the first step along the way to becoming fishers of men. That is what the disciples did. They simply opened their hearts to Jesus and, whether they understood him fully or not, they became effective fishers of men.

THURSDAY 5 SEPTEMBER
EVIL SPIRITS

READING MARK 1:21–34
'"Be quiet!" said Jesus sternly. "Come out of him!" The evil spirit shook the man violently and came out of him with a shriek . . . That evening after sunset the people brought to Jesus all the sick and demon-possessed . . . and Jesus healed many' (vv. 25,26,32,34a, NIV).

ONE MAN demanded the whole of Jesus' attention in the synagogue. The man was possessed by an evil spirit. What that means is very difficult to say. Spirit possession is almost impossible to define. Sometimes it seems to be used as a convenient label for violent mental disorders which could be described in other ways. But, however we define our terms, there are some situations where a person becomes detached from reality and has to be reached via an outside influence, that is to say the evil spirit.

No amount of reason will help. They are beyond the reach of normal conversation. The only way through is by prayer and by the authority of Christ himself. A clear distinction is made by Mark between casting out demons and the general run of Jesus' healing ministry. It is therefore tempting to think of casting out demons as something quite separate from other kinds of healing, however it takes place.

Mark 9:29 & 27

God's power is involved in exorcism, as when Jesus cast the evil spirit out of this man. God's power is involved in spiritual healing of all kinds. God's power is involved in physical healing, as when Jesus healed Peter's mother-in-law. God's power is involved in physical healing of all kinds.

The healing performed by Jesus was remarkable, visible, often instantaneous, and usually we call it miraculous. But the same power is at work in all healing. What was available through Jesus is available to us, the healing power of God.

TO PONDER

FRIDAY 6 SEPTEMBER
THE SOLITARY PLACE

READING MARK 1:35–45
'Jesus got up, left the house and went off to a solitary place, where he prayed ... A man with leprosy came to him and begged him on his knees, "If you are willing, you can make me clean"' (vv. 35b,40, NIV).

ALBERT SCHWEITZER, the famous musician, doctor and Christian missionary to Central Africa claimed that Mark's gospel consists of many separate sections, like stations on a railway system between which there are no connecting trains! He felt that each incident related by Mark was complete in itself. He could see no follow-through from one incident to the next in any clear order. In one sense he may be right. We cannot use Mark's gospel to construct a biography of Jesus, or even an account of his ministry in time sequence. However, there *are* connections between incidents. Sometimes the connections are theological ones. Sometimes the connections have to do with subject matter, as when parables are recorded together, miracles set side by side and so on.

4:1–34;
7:24–8:26

One of the connections between the two incidents in today's passage is isolation. Jesus prayed alone. The leper lived alone, cut off from the crowd by his dreaded disease. Jesus searched for isolation, the leper had it forced upon him. What a difference!

On holiday the lonely majesty of remote mountains is a joy to be dreamt about for the rest of the year. We rejoice at the splendid scenery, at the quiet calm or even the roaring wind. But the dream quickly becomes a nightmare when the mist descends and we are left on the mountain unable to return to base. Isolation oppresses us and fills us with fear.

TO PONDER *Unsought isolation in remote regions may be hard to bear. The lot of the leper, the AIDS sufferer, or in many cases of one who is simply old and forgotten, shunned by the crowd, and isolated from those around them is still harder to cope with. May we extend to them the hand of true friendship.*

SATURDAY 7 SEPTEMBER
SHOCKING!

READING MARK 2:13–22
'As he walked along, he saw Levi son of Alphaeus sitting at the tax collector's booth. "Follow me," Jesus told him, and Levi got up and followed him' (v. 14, NIV).

IT IS ALMOST IMPOSSIBLE to shock people these days. Newspaper headlines become increasingly hideous as they vie for circulation, trying to draw our attention with short, forceful phrases which will stop us in our tracks. But a phrase which disgusts us this year becomes common currency the next.

Something similar happens with the gospel story. We cease to be shocked by the people involved. Jesus called a tax-collector. That seems innocent enough, but tax-collectors in those days were traitors who had sold their services to the Roman oppressor. Nowadays the gutter press would have a field day with that one. They would describe the tax man in foul and abusive language. They would condemn Jesus and point Levi out as a scandalous traitor, the lowest of the low, fit only to be despised and spat on. A man who would keep company with a thug like Levi, let alone make him one of his disciples, would be fit to be described in the vilest language of condemnation.

How easily we forget how hard it was for respectable people to accept Jesus. How easily we forget that Jesus really did keep company with the lowest of the low. He did not try to save his reputation in any way at all. For many centuries his Church has been one of the pillars of the establishment, giving authority to the respectable, keeping things stable and secure. But that was not the way of Jesus, and when some of his people follow his way, we may find it shocking.

Think of the worst person you know and to say to yourself, 'He (or she) is just as fit as I am to keep company with Christ.' Then ask yourself what you are doing to bring them into fellowship with Christ.

FOR THOUGHT

SUNDAY 8 SEPTEMBER
TWO OFFENCES

READING MARK 2:1–12, 23–28
'Son, your sins are forgiven' (v. 5b, NIV).
'So the Son of Man is Lord even of the Sabbath' (v. 28, NIV).

GOD SAID, 'Let us make man in our image, in our likeness, and let them rule over . . . all the earth' (Gen 1:26). Jesus took this Old Testament statement seriously. He accepted that God had given man control of the earth. Such control includes the institutions God has provided for our benefit.

One of those institutions is the Sabbath. The Son of Man, says Jesus, is in control of the Sabbath. It is for man to use the Sabbath to the best advantage. The Sabbath is to be a blessing, not a curse. Such thinking was in line with the best Jewish thought and scholarship of Jesus' day. So possibly those who heard Jesus claim authority over the Sabbath would have listened and accepted his words, if only he hadn't already offended them by saying he could forgive sins.

That, in the eyes of the devout men who criticised Jesus, was unforgivable. To claim to be able to forgive sins was the height of blasphemy. Who can forgive sins but God alone? Of course God alone can forgive sins, but in another sense the answer is also all of us. We can forgive. And by forgiving we play a part in God's great work of reconciliation. We each participate in the great forgiveness which God offers freely through Christ Jesus. What a privilege! What a responsibility!

TO PONDER: *When tempted to harbour a grievance against someone today, however justified that grievance may be, let us remember that forgiving the one who has offended us is part of God's great work of salvation in Christ.*

PRAYER SUBJECT: *For a right attitude to Sunday.*

PRAYER: *Thank you, God, for Sunday. Thank you for rest, recreation, and worship. Help us to spread the benefits of Sunday to all sections of our community, so that others will be encouraged to worship too.*

MONDAY 9 SEPTEMBER
UNHOLY ALLIANCE

READING MARK 3:1–12
'Then the Pharisees went out and began to plot with the Herodians how they might kill Jesus' (v. 6, NIV).

ILL-FOUNDED CRITICISM can easily turn to malice. Pharisees were reasonable men, pillars of society, concerned to uphold worthwhile standards and traditions which had been attacked for centuries.

Naturally they thought Jesus' claim to forgive sins blasphemous. They were shocked at the company Jesus kept, and by his disciples' sabbath-breaking. We need not even be surprised that they thought Jesus should wait till the next day instead of healing a non-urgent case on the Sabbath. The Pharisees' criticism of Jesus was ill-founded, but at least it was sincere. However, once the ill-founded criticism caught hold, it was only a short step to making an unholy alliance with the Herodians.

2:7
2:16
2:23

3:1

Herod symbolised everything the Pharisees opposed. His power was Roman. He himself was Idumaean, hardly Jewish at all. He married his brother's wife – against Jewish law and custom, then was completely dominated by her. His followers opposed Jesus simply because they saw him as a political threat, very different from the opposition of the Pharisees.

Sometimes we must join forces with our opponents. This is always costly, on occasion just costing pride, but in this instance costing integrity. The Pharisees should have avoided all contact with the corruption of the Herodians.

Don't condemn, but consider. Do we ever join forces with opponents to gain some greater objective? Such co-operation can be positively good, but have we ever, for the sake of ease, allowed ourselves to become involved in things of which we were later ashamed? TO PONDER

TUESDAY 10 SEPTEMBER
WITH HIM

READING MARK 3:13–19
'He appointed twelve–designating them apostles – that they might be with him and that he might send them out to preach and to have authority to drive out demons. These are the twelve . . . Simon the Zealot and Judas Iscariot' (vv. 14,15,16a,18b,19a, NIV).

WoL 4 Sep
WoL 7 Sep
v. 18

A MOTLEY CREW is just about the only way to describe the twelve whom Jesus called to be with him. Most were fishermen. Some were not. We have already commented on becoming fishers of men; we have already commented on the tax collector, but what are we to make of Jesus calling a Zealot?

The Zealots were men committed to overthrow Roman occupation by whatever means that might be achieved. At the outset they were idealists, committed to the betterment of society, but they ultimately degenerated into a body of mere assassins, called Sicarii.* For Jesus to keep company with a Zealot was like having an active member of the IRA amongst the apostles. If we were shocked by Jesus calling a 'quisling' tax-collector, how much more shocked we should be by this man of war amongst the Twelve.

It was no wonder the authorities thought Jesus was a dangerous revolutionary. It was hard for them to understand that twelve people like the men whom Jesus chose could have as their main aim a preaching and teaching ministry which would drive out demons, rather than drive forward political aims. It is equally hard for many today to see the Church as a spiritual entity, and not just a political one.

TO PONDER

People of all political persuasions, or of none, may be Christ's disciples. But the purpose of Christian discipleship is spiritual. Unless spiritual aims take precedence over political endeavours, Christ's disciples and the Christian Church cannot reach their full potential.

*Sicarii = Sword-bearers (New Westminster Dictionary of the Bible, Philadelphia, 1974.)

WEDNESDAY 11 SEPTEMBER
NO FAVOURITES

READING MARK 3:20–21, 31–35
'A crowd gathered, so that he and his disciples were not even able to eat. When his family heard about this, they went to take charge of him, for they said, "He is out of his mind"' (vv. 20b,21, NIV).

FAMILY TIES ARE IMPORTANT. We need support, care and encouragement from the cradle onwards. Without it we become physical, emotional or spiritual cripples. No better way has been found to give such care than within a family.

A family is a unit where there is commitment to each other, concern for each other and freedom from each other. The purpose of close family ties is not to keep the family together at all costs for all time, but to give necessary support for the children of the family to make their way within a wider community, becoming independent, and in many instances establishing new families for the care and support of the next generation.

The original family then becomes a resource or refuge, not a reformatory. It is not an institution of justice, controlling offenders and attempting to socialise them all over again. Jesus' family failed to understand this. They wanted to hang on to Jesus, to restrict him and keep him to themselves, instead of giving him up to the wider community.

Naturally, they also wanted privileged access to Jesus. In some situations that would be appropriate. Later, from the cross, Jesus' special concern was for his mother, but not on this occasion. Jesus was creating his own family, the family of God where there are no special favourites. In the divine community, the Christian community where Jesus is in control, we all have the same standing. We are all brothers and sisters in Christ.

Despite our inequalities, God has no favourites. We are all guilty sinners whose guilt has been taken away. TO PONDER

THURSDAY 12 SEPTEMBER
UNFORGIVABLE

READING MARK 3:22–30
'If a house is divided against itself, that house cannot stand ... Whoever blasphemes against the Holy Spirit will never be forgiven' (vv. 25,29a, NIV).

John 4:24

SCANDALOUS DIVISIONS within the Church weaken witness and dissipate energy. It is important to know what we believe. It is important to worship correctly 'in spirit and in truth'. But it is vital to remember that people have different perceptions of the truth. Fighting our own corner, trying to make people believe every detail of *our* belief, detracts from the urgent task of spreading the gospel of Jesus Christ. The gospel is not merely belief, but encounter. It is meeting with Christ, relating to God who speaks to us through his Holy Spirit.

What, then, of the sin against the Holy Spirit? Such sin is not one act or even a series of acts. It is an attitude of mind. It creeps up on us gradually. We do something wrong, and pretend we haven't. We do it again, and it doesn't seem so bad. We continue to do it, and finally we may convince ourselves it is right! That is how we come to commit the unforgivable sin. We convince ourselves that right is wrong and wrong is right. We cannot be forgiven, for we no longer have any sense of sin.

The surest way to avoid committing the unforgivable sin is to keep Christ central in our thinking. When we concentrate on him we remain sensitive to right and wrong. Sometimes we will be puzzled as to which course of action to take. Sometimes we may have doubts. But we shall never reach the point where we blindly keep on doing wrong, deceiving ourselves into thinking it is right. Differences with our Christian neighbours may remain, but we will get them in proportion. We will fight the common enemy, Satan, instead of fighting each other.

TO PONDER *Only those who no longer have a conscience can be guilty of the unforgivable sin.*

FRIDAY 13 SEPTEMBER
RESPONSE

READING MARK 4:1–9
'Some fell on rocky places, where it did not have much soil. It sprang up quickly, because the soil was shallow. But when the sun came up, the plants were scorched, and they withered because they had no root' (vv. 5,6, NIV).

SOWING IS A RISKY BUSINESS. Modern agricultural methods have taken much of the uncertainty out of sowing. In many places seed is no longer scattered by hand, almost indiscriminately, as it was in Jesus' day. But shallow soil is still used. Indeed, as more and more 'marginal' land is ploughed up, as more and more forest is felled to make way for grassland, Jesus' picture of a quick but shallow response takes on a chilling relevance in today's world.

The shallow soils of tropical rain forests can support life in abundance, if there is sufficient tree cover. Cut down the trees and for a few seasons there will be crops galore. Prosperity seems within reach – and then it all goes sour. The shallow soil is exhausted. Attempts to eke out a living on it begin to fail, and the final condition is worse than the first. It is a tragic picture, all too often repeated. It will take massive international efforts of education, economic aid and scientific study in order to reverse the horrendous decline into desert conditions.

Luke 11:26

Woe betide us if we allow a similar shallowness in our Christian life. All the rich resources of Christ and his Church are open to us, if we will only grasp hold of them. When we hear the word of the Lord, through our daily reading, through worship alongside other Christians, or through sensitive contact with all kinds of people in our daily life, we need to do more than to respond with unthinking enthusiasm. New insights may trigger an instant response. But that response has to be deepened and strengthened continually, like the gradual rooting of the forest over the centuries. Response to Christ is the task of a lifetime.

Destruction takes a moment. Construction takes eternity. TO PONDER

SATURDAY 14 SEPTEMBER
PARABLES

READING MARK 4:10–20
'Jesus said to them, "Don't you understand this parable? How then will you understand any parable?"' (v. 13, NIV).

PARABLES ARE INFURIATING. They are so simple – yet perplexingly profound. They drive home a point – and raise a myriad questions in our minds. They make the truth clear – and hide it from us. They bring us face to face with Jesus – and put a barrier between us, for they require the effort of interpretation.

Some of the barriers are barriers of time. Conditions have changed since the days of Jesus. Vast populations have lost contact with the land so that, in many instances, Jesus' illustrations no longer strike an immediate chord. But even in Jesus' own day his parables fell on deaf ears. They puzzled his disciples, whose Jewish background probably caused them to read more into the simple stories than they were meant to. Some scholars see this tendency in the explanation given of the parable of the sower. They think that it is an interpretation added at a later date, rather than one spoken by Jesus at the time.

That may be so. The scholars could be right, and the simple message of this parable may not be in the complicated interpretations of the different kinds of soil. It may indeed have a simple message that whatever happens, if the word is preached (sown), there will be a harvest. But at the same time, the explanation given in this chapter of Mark is a helpful one. Each of us can identify with one of the responses mentioned. We each know whether we have allowed the gospel to take root in us, to shape our lives and govern our actions. Reminders about the power of Satan, the shallow enthusiasms which drive us all over the place, and the cares of the world which prise us away from our contact with Jesus, are all timely.

v. 15
v. 17
v. 19

TO PONDER *The gospel is simple. Its detail is profound.*

SUNDAY 15 SEPTEMBER
LETTING OUT THE LIGHT

READING MARK 4:21–34
'Then he asked them, "When someone lights a lamp, does he put a box over it to shut out the light? Of course not! The light couldn't be seen or used. A lamp is placed on a stand to shine and be useful.
'"All that is now hidden will someday come to light"' (vv. 21, 22, LB).

TRUTH WILL OUT, and truth can be devastating. How many of us can honestly say that our lives contain nothing which, if it was publicly known, would either embarrass us deeply, cause us to lose face or even, in some instances, destroy us?

Naturally, criminals like to cover the light. (John 3:19,20). Bright light is one of the burglar's worst enemies. But wrong-doers aren't alone in sometimes wishing to cover the light. New street lighting was recently installed in our little road. What a blessing! It makes us feel safer, helps us to see our way clearly, makes tripping on the uneven pavement less likely, and helps us to avoid treading in unpleasant messes. Yet many complained that the lights were too bright, and could stop people sleeping!

We human beings do not always welcome the light. It makes us uncomfortable. We may prefer to remain in a cosy little world, blotting out the light which could reveal awkward truths, and which might goad us into activity. But Christ calls on Christians not to hide their lamps. We have the light, so let us take the risk of spreading it. It will reveal some things we don't like. Some things, we may feel, are better to remain hidden, yet people can only enjoy the benefits of the light if it is uncovered. Let none of us be fearful or ashamed to witness to the light Christ has brought into our lives.

TO PONDER: *How important it is for Christians to witness. Let our witness be muted, and soon the opportunity to witness will no longer exist.*

PRAYER SUBJECT: *For courage to witness.*

PRAYER: *Forgive me, Lord, for the times when I have been afraid to witness to the power and effect of the gospel in my life. Give me courage to tell others what Christ means to me.*

MONDAY 16 SEPTEMBER
THE ACTUAL WORDS

READING MARK 4:35–41
'Jesus stood up and commanded the wind, "Be quiet!" and he said to the waves, "Be still!" The wind died down, and there was a great calm. Then Jesus said to his disciples, "Why are you frightened? Have you still no faith?"' (vv. 39,40, GNB).

MARK'S GOSPEL IS DIRECT. Mark uses the present tense over and over again when he describes the scene of Jesus' actions.* This gives great urgency to the message. He uses few connecting words. Those that he uses are simple. And in today's passage, Mark alone reports Jesus' command to the wind and waves as direct speech. The other gospels say that Jesus gave an order to the winds and waves. Only Mark reports directly what that order was. Jesus simply said, 'Be quiet!' 'Be still!' No magic formulas were used. Plain, direct speech was sufficient.

v. 39
compare
Luke 8:24b &
Matt 8:26b

Why would Mark stress this? Surely he is concerned to bring comfort to the Church here and now. The storms which Jesus quells are not just the storms of ancient Galilee, but the storms of the church in Rome in Mark's day, or of present day London and New York, of Bucharest and Beijing, of the opulent church and the poor struggling congregation, of groups of secret Christians united in a common struggle, and of high-profile communities whose internal strife is there for all to see.

The calm and order which Jesus brings are of particular comfort to small, struggling minorities. If Jesus could calm the winds and waves, and – an even greater miracle – the frights and fears of his disciples, he can do the same for us.

TO PONDER *Mark . . . makes it clear that winds and waves of the church's oppression are powerless to harm the little ship in which Christ's disciples travel. There is still a great calm once he who is with them in the boat arises to speak peace.*

(R. P. Martin)

*This is not apparent, except in the original Greek. Most translations turn present into past.

TUESDAY 17 SEPTEMBER
POSSESSED

READING MARK 5:1–10
'He shouted at the top of his voice, "What do you want with me, Jesus, Son of the Most High God? Swear to God that you won't torture me!" For Jesus had said to him, "Come out of this man, you evil spirit!"' (vv. 7,8, NIV).

EVIL SPIRITS figure strongly in Mark's gospel. We have met one possessed man in the synagogue. Here we meet one in the cemetery, still a religious setting, but a wild scene, on the shores of the lake so recently wracked by a violent storm. Among the tombstones, as the shadows lengthened in the evening, the spirits of the dead would seem very close. How easily tombstones can convey an atmosphere of evil and foreboding! Small wonder that the longer the man spent there, the more he became possessed. Cutting him off from the community, consigning him to the tombs was probably the worst possible thing in his unfortunate state. He could only deteriorate.

1:23

4:35–41

But tragically, the worse he got the more attached he became to his fallen state. A little like the leper, isolated, unable to believe Jesus wanted to help him, this poor demoniac was so cut off that he could not face the possibility of being brought back into the real world.

1:40

The evil spirits possessed him, in much the same way as addiction completely possesses the addict, so that in many instances there is no desire for deliverance from it. Once again, Jesus uses no magic formula, only a simple command. At first it was ineffective. The demoniac thought he was being tortured! A more personal approach was required. Jesus asked him his name. It sounds simple. It is simple. We rarely come across such instant results in our own dealings with people. But our response still needs to be modelled on that of Jesus. Simple speaking, and personal attention.

The possessed man was healed immediately. Three years of intense, exhausting effort on the part of Jesus still didn't produce perfect disciples.

TO PONDER

WEDNESDAY 18 SEPTEMBER
FEAR

READING MARK 5:11–20
'Those tending the pigs ran off . . . When they came to Jesus, they saw the man who had been possessed by the legion of demons, sitting there, dressed and in his right mind; and they were afraid' (vv. 14a,15, NIV).

FOR YEARS the pig minders had herded their pigs close to the tombs, aware of the shrieks and the fearsome gestures of the possessed man. Probably they had fed him scraps, leaving them where they knew he would find them, never venturing too close in case he turned his violence onto them.

We can understand that when the pigs suddenly scurried down the hillside into the lake, as the price of the man's sanity, the men were terrified. We can understand them running off. We can understand them bringing their friends. But why would they be so afraid when they saw the man, dressed and in his right mind? Surely, that should have been the point at which their fears were allayed, and they became calm. Instead, at that very moment they asked Jesus to go away from them.

v. 15

Mark makes it appear that their distress over the loss of the pigs was greater than their joy over the sanity of the man. Economic factors outweighed humanitarian issues. Or were they simply terrified by Jesus' power? If he could restore the madman, what sort of power might he have over them? Might he not upset their lives completely?

Yet again we see that Jesus did not, and indeed could not, use miracles to make people believe. Fear of change is a powerful human emotion so that sometimes, instead of bringing belief, miracles may engender fear.

TO PONDER *When we overcome our fear, and let Jesus take control, our lives will indeed be changed completely. Take that risk. Allow Jesus to direct your life, and see the change that follows.*

THURSDAY 19 SEPTEMBER
YOUR FAITH

READING MARK 5:21–34
'He said to her, "Daughter, your faith has healed you. Go in peace and be freed from your suffering"' (v. 34, NIV).

FAITH IS THE FOUNDATION of our spiritual life. It stems from God, but in a deep sense faith is also ours. It is a gift given to us by God, to use, to develop and to nurture just like all his other gifts. One of the uses of faith is for healing. Jesus, as we have already seen, went about healing. Right from the start of the gospel story in Mark healing occurs, coming from the hand of Jesus.

Sometimes, as when demons are cast out, the healing takes place regardless of any faith the person involved might exercise. Indeed, this must be so, for one result of demon possession is surely an inability to exercise faith. You can't be committed to God as well as possessed by demons. Demons may believe in God, but they do not exercise faith in God, for faith is not simply belief. It is belief plus commitment.

1:24; 5:7–10 etc.

Rom 5:1; 12:1

On other occasions, too, Mark disregards the faith of the person being healed, as though it could well be irrelevant. Sometimes, as with the palsied man, faith on someone else's behalf effects the cure. But in a number of instances healing seems to depend completely on the faith of the person being healed. Such was the case on this occasion.

8:22ff.
2:1ff.
7:26–30
1:40; 10:52

It must have been a shock to the woman, to be told that her faith had healed her. She naturally assumed healing had come from Jesus. Many times she had placed her trust in others to heal her, and they could not. The one time that she found someone who could heal her, she is told that it is her own faith that has worked the cure.

Faith involves relying on Jesus – and developing the gifts God has given us, one of which is indeed faith.

TO PONDER
1 Cor 12:9

FRIDAY 20 SEPTEMBER
CONTINUING FAITH

READING MARK 5:35–43
'Ignoring what they said, Jesus told the synagogue ruler, "Don't be afraid; just believe"' (v. 36, NIV).

JAIRUS WAS NEAR DESPAIR. His daughter was mortally sick, yet Jesus stopped to pay attention to a woman who was now perfectly well. What a wrong sense of priorities! Surely the well woman could go her own way in peace, and let Jesus hurry to the daughter who was sick and close to death.

What a blow, after this delay, to get the news his daughter had died! Only when this message had been received did Jesus say 'Don't be afraid; just believe.' Already Jairus had exercised faith by coming to Jesus. He had taken action. He had put himself completely in the Master's hands. His faith had been disappointed.

When you trust someone and they appear to fail, nothing is harder than continuing to trust. Yet that's what Jairus was being asked to do, to trust a failure. His daughter was dead, beyond reach. Nothing could save her now. Yet still Jairus trusted. He stayed alongside Jesus, who proceeded without panic. Imagine Jairus's anguish, when he heard the people wailing. Imagine the conflicting thoughts running through his mind when he heard Jesus saying that the child was not dead but asleep.

'Who was right? Jesus or the people? How did Jesus know? What could he do? Could all these people possibly be wrong? How had he got himself into this mess? Might it have been better not to bother Jesus at all, and just accept that God had taken his daughter to be with him?' Jairus must have felt thoroughly confused. And in his confusion – he trusted.

TO PONDER *Jairus did not have all the answers. He didn't know his daughter would live. He continued to put himself in the hands of Jesus, an apparent failure. If we do the same, like Jairus, we will not be finally disappointed.*

SATURDAY 21 SEPTEMBER
FAILURE

READING MARK 6:1–13
'"Isn't this the carpenter? Isn't this Mary's son and the brother of James, Joseph, Judas and Simon? Aren't his sisters here with us?" And they took offence at him . . . He could not do any miracles there' (vv. 3,5a, NIV).

RAISING THE DEAD was the ultimate success. Mark follows this with a record of failure. The connection between success and failure is strong. Whenever anything is attempted both possibilities are there. For Jesus, too, success was not guaranteed. His God-given power could be thwarted by simple prejudice and antagonism.

At Nazareth they knew Jesus' background. They knew there was something doubtful about his birth. They knew he was just a carpenter. They knew he hadn't studied in Jerusalem, or gone through the training of a Rabbi. His education had been with them, close at hand – and possibly not even very remarkable. We don't know if he was regarded as a clever lad in Nazareth. His disputation with the learned men took place in Jerusalem, not at home.

John 7:15

Luke 2:46,47

At Nazareth they could not accept him for what he was. They could only see what, to them, he had been. We all do it. And we all suffer because of it. Prejudice blinds us to a person's true worth. It may be their colour, their sex, their riches, or poverty, their youth or their age. It may even be their height or the way they do their hair which alters our attitude towards them. And so we lose the benefits of many with real gifts, like Jesus, and suffer from charlatans who have the right appearance, an unknown background, or an origin that seems right. We force failure on to people, or force them to be remote from us if they are to succeed.

Think of someone in your congregation, whom you consider unfit for their responsibility. Then ask yourself, is it my attitude, thinking them incapable, which holds them back? The answer will probably be yes!

TO PONDER

SUNDAY 22 SEPTEMBER
FALSE HONOUR

READING MARK 6:14–29
'Herod feared John and protected him, knowing him to be a righteous and holy man. When Herod heard John, he was greatly puzzled; yet he liked to listen to him' (v. 20, NIV).

HEROD WAS FASCINATED by John the Baptist. John was a dangerous opponent, so Herod imprisoned him. Herod was no fool. To maintain his precarious position of power he had to be able to judge men's characters. He needed the ability to make snap decisions when the odds were against him. He had to know when someone was bluffing, and when they meant what they said.

Herod had to keep his opponents guessing. By contrast, John was so clear, so honest, so uncompromising, that in spite of putting him in prison, Herod had to listen to him, almost mesmerised by his condemnation of everything Herod stood for. It would have been the easiest thing in the world for Herod to execute John, but he could not bring himself to destroy the one who brought him his only contact with things that were pure and true.

Herod's wife saw the danger. She saw the king almost hypnotised by John's persuasive honesty. And she used the king's sense of honour to trick him into beheading the Baptist. Mark tells the story clearly. We see the king's dilemma. But it was not just a case of a weak man dominated by a strong woman. Once a vow was made, he was honour-bound to keep it. Jephthah, centuries before, had succumbed to this false sense of honour, and had sacrificed his own daughter because of a foolish vow (Judges 11:30). How careful we need to be when making promises, not to allow ourselves to be needlessly led into situations that we cannot control.

PRAYER SUBJECT: *For the power to keep our promises.*

PRAYER: *Dear Father in Heaven, may we always speak the truth. Help us to keep the promises we make to others, and to you. Help us to make the right promises. Keep us from foolish pledges which cause harm to others and to ourselves.*

MONDAY 23 SEPTEMBER
MIRACULOUS MISSION

READING MARK 6:30–44
'His disciples . . . said, "It is already very late, and this is a lonely place. Send the people away, and let them go to the nearby farms and villages in order to buy themselves something to eat." "You yourselves give them something to eat," Jesus answered' (vv.35b–37a, GNB).

THE DISCIPLES SAW TROUBLE ahead. A hungry crowd would grow restless. Instead of sitting, listening to Jesus with rapt attention, they would start to complain. Crowd control – probably the job of the disciples – would become increasingly difficult. So the sensible course of action was to send the crowd away, and let them fend for themselves, buying food wherever they could.

But that was not Jesus' way. He told his disciples to look after the crowd, and feed them. It was a tall order. Five thousand people could not be fed just like that, but they did as they were told. They researched the situation rapidly, going out to see what they could find. Jesus supplemented their efforts with the greatest miracle of all, the only one mentioned in all four gospels – and indeed doubly mentioned by Matthew and Mark.

Matt 14:13–21
Luke 9:10–17
John 6:1–10 cf.
Mark 8:1–10
Matt 15:32–39

As I write, there is crisis in the Gulf. Refugees are flooding across the borders into Jordan, Turkey and Iran. The problem threatens to become a disaster of horrendous size. Jesus' message to the world community is to feed these people. Action must be taken. Once it is in hand, then the Lord will add his power and his resources to ours. But unless we obey and make the first compassionate move, hunger will turn to starvation, to unrest and ultimately to war.

TO PONDER

By now you probably know the outcome of the crisis just described. Has your contribution to that outcome been a positive or negative one, through your attitude and/or your practical action?

TUESDAY 24 SEPTEMBER
OUR ADVANTAGE

READING MARK 6:45–56
'The disciples were completely amazed, because they had not understood the real meaning of the feeding of the five thousand; their minds could not grasp it' (vv. 51b,52, GNB).

WE'RE ALL IN THE SAME BOAT as the disciples. Our minds can't grasp the whole meaning of what Jesus did. He fed the multitudes. He walked on the water. He stilled the storm. No wonder the disciples could not take it in. No wonder that we ourselves stand back in amazement.

v. 52
But where the disciples did not understand because their minds were darkened or, as NIV puts it, 'their hearts were hardened,' surely we have the advantage over them. We ought to be able to understand. We have the benefit of knowing the story of Jesus' passion, death and resurrection. We know of the coming of the Spirit. We have experienced the power of the Church not just in Mark's day, but the power of almost two thousand years of spiritual witness; two thousand years of sharing the grace of God through the ministry of his servants, Christians of all generations with varying degrees of understanding.

Matt 28:20
Acts 1:8 etc.
Jesus indeed calls on us to continue to feed the multitudes. He calls on us to keep on healing the sick by any and every means possible. He calls on us above all to continue to preach the Word that Jesus is Lord.

A VERSE
Forth in thy name, O Lord, I go
My daily labour to pursue,
Thee, only thee, resolved to know
In all I think, or speak, or do.

Thee may I set at my right hand,
Whose eyes my inmost purpose see;
And labour on at thy command,
And offer all my works to thee.
(Charles Wesley, SASB 667, HFTC 306)

WEDNESDAY 25 SEPTEMBER
RELIGION AND HYGIENE

READING MARK 7:1–13
'"Why don't your disciples live according to the tradition of the elders instead of eating their food with 'unclean' hands?"
He replied, "Isaiah was right when he prophesied about you hypocrites; as it is written, 'These people honour me with their lips, but their hearts are far from me'"' (vv. 5b,6 NIV).

TEACHERS OF THE LAW get a bad press in Mark. Mark's gospel contains little, if anything, good about them. They were experts in religion who controlled the day-to-day life of the people. Presumably most were sincere, educated men who wanted to do the very best they could with the knowledge they had. But, instead of looking at the motives behind actions, like lawyers the world over they could only look at the actions themselves.

When lawyers do start looking into motive things get difficult, for no one can fully gauge what another person's intention is. In Britain, for example, if a car kills someone on the road, the law requires a jury to decide what the driver's intention was when they took the action which caused death. That, of course, is almost impossible. So quite often a driver who kills by careless driving is convicted of a minor offence, and simply fined.

Recently the mother of a man who had been killed by a car saw this car parked a few days later. In rage she took a hammer to it. She was fined the same amount as the driver who had killed her son, but additionally she received a suspended prison sentence! The car, she claims, was looked on as more valuable than her son's life. Such are the difficulties which will arise when intention is brought to bear upon the legal system.

In spite of the difficulties, Christ calls us to be more careful about motives than about actions themselves. TO PONDER

THURSDAY 26 SEPTEMBER
CLEANSING

READING MARK 7:14–23
'"Don't you see that nothing that enters a man from the outside can make him 'unclean'? For it doesn't go into his heart but into his stomach, and then out of his body"' (vv. 18b,19, NIV).

ON SATURDAY it will be ninety six years since Louis Pasteur died. He and his contemporaries revolutionised our thinking about infection, the need for hygiene to prevent infection spreading, and the importance of uncontaminated water. Little more than a hundred years ago people still debated whether bacteria even existed. Microscopes had shown them up at a much earlier stage, but what they were and how they worked was quite a recent discovery.

We know WHY things have to be clean. It is not just a matter of looking nice, avoiding the discomfort of dust and dirt, of keeping religious taboos, or trying to be one up on the neighbours. It is a matter of making sure that unseen, living organisms do not invade us and cause unnecessary illness. Cleanliness, piped water and proper sewage disposal probably save more lives than all the antibiotics put together.

So we find it hard to take on board Jesus' words that nothing entering from outside can make us unclean. Today's generation is as confused as the Pharisees were with regard to physical and spiritual cleansing. Many of the things we see make us feel contaminated. We can't avoid contact with the world's corrupting influences. But whatever influences affect us, we are assured that God's Holy Spirit is available, powerful and strong to protect us.

TO PONDER *We determine whether we open ourselves to the purifying, cleansing power of the Holy Spirit, which expresses itself in noble thoughts and actions, or whether we remain chained to the spirits of the age, which express*
vv. 21–23 *themselves in envy, slander, arrogance and folly.*

FRIDAY 27 SEPTEMBER
ONE GENTILE WOMAN

READING MARK 7:24–30
'Jesus left that place and went to the vicinity of Tyre. He entered a house and did not want anyone to know it; yet he could not keep his presence secret . . . a woman whose little daughter was possessed by an evil spirit came and fell at his feet. The woman was a Greek' (vv. 24–26, NIV).

JESUS WAS SURROUNDED by crowds. His attempt to get away from them earlier had failed, and now some time later he was trying to get even further way by going into country which was beyond the accepted bounds of Israel. Tyre is in Lebanon. In those days there would be a considerable number of Jews in the area, but it was basically Gentile. Jesus thought he would be able to remain unrecognised amongst the Gentiles. But it was not to be. Immediately she heard he was there, a Gentile woman found him and begged him to heal her demon-possessed daughter.

6:32,33

Jesus' reaction to the request seems harsh and narrow in outlook. It was the natural reaction of a tired minister who had a definite mission, and felt he was being pressured to go beyond that mission. It was hardly a considered statement of policy. Jesus must have had some idea that his mission would spread. But his immediate task was, forlornly, to try to convince his own people.

But the gospel cannot be limited in such a way. The woman's clever rejoinder to Jesus' impulsive reply reminded him that God's love cannot be limited. Thankful for such a reminder, Jesus assured the woman her daughter would be healed, and the demon left her.

Jesus' human reactions were normal. He became tired. He reacted to situations impulsively. He took all the risks of becoming human. But he was prepared to listen, to learn, and to widen his vision when prompted by the most unlikely people.

TO PONDER

SATURDAY 28 SEPTEMBER
WHY SO SECRET?

READING MARK 7:31–37; 8:22–26,30
'Through Sidon, down to the Sea of Galilee and into the region of Decapolis . . . Jesus commanded them not to tell anyone.' (7:31,36a, NIV).
'They came to Bethsaida . . . Jesus sent him home, saying, "Don't go into the village" . . . Jesus warned them not to tell anyone about him' (8:22a,26,30, NIV).

DON'T TELL! Keep it quiet! Stay away from the village where gossip may start! Over and over again Jesus told people not to spread the word that he had healed them. Why ever should this be? Some think it is just Mark's way of explaining why Jesus wasn't immediately hailed as Messiah. But there must be more to it than that.

Matt 11:4
Luke 7:22
6:7,13
Matt 10:42

Surely Jesus did not want to be followed simply as a wonder-worker. His mission was to heal. He gives his disciples authority to heal. He tells us to continue his practical ministry. But that must never be the prime purpose of Christian ministry. The prime purpose is to bring people into contact with God, to introduce them, not to the temporary healing of body or mind, but to an eternal, spiritual relationship with God.

Healing is fine, but it is only a temporary expedient. It keeps the inevitable end at bay for a while longer. The one sure thing for us all, whether we are healed miraculously, delivered from demon possession, or brought back from the dead, is that we shall all die. How important, then, to foster a right relationship with God, not based on physical healing, but on the eternal things of the Spirit. When we offer the gospel to people primarily as a means to physical or mental healing, we do the gospel an injustice.

TO PONDER *Christ brings healing – and more, much more besides. He brings redemptive suffering. He brings a questioning mind, a heart open to God and a life which is full in spite of, or even because of, our physical limitations.*

SUNDAY 29 SEPTEMBER
BREAD FOR ALL

READING MARK 8:1–10
'During those days another large crowd gathered. Since they had nothing to eat, Jesus called his disciples to him and said, "I have compassion for these people . . . If I send them home hungry, they will collapse on the way"' (vv. 1–3, NIV).

THE HUNGRY MUST BE FED. It is a simple statement. It is Christian. It is compassionate. It is difficult to achieve. There are always more and more mouths to feed. The hungry far away can be kept out of mind, despite the insistent clamour of the media. The hungry close at hand can be rationalised almost out of existence in countries where any semblance of a welfare state remains. Yet we all live with the uneasy feeling that we should be doing something more than we are doing to alleviate the world's hunger, and a sense of powerlessness even to scratch the surface of the problem.

Jesus' two feeding miracles were also scratching at the surface of the problem. They did not solve it. Temporarily, several thousand people were fed. The next day they were hungry again. Like physical healing, miraculous feeding is only a temporary measure. It doesn't solve the problems of the world. Aid programmes, economic and political reforms, education, scientific research into new and better strains of food crops – these are the measures which will feed the hungry in today's world. Jesus' action was a symbolic gesture. It was a forcible reminder that the hungry must be fed.

And this second feeding incident took place during the days Jesus spent outside Jewish territory. He was, in a sense, on foreign soil. Feeding the hungry close at hand is good. It is also essential to feed the hungry far away. That must be the aid of research, not just to produce surpluses in the developed world, but to provide ongoing resources for all the world's population.

PRAYER SUBJECT: *For food.*

PRAYER: *Thank you, Father, for the abundance and variety of food you have provided for our needs. Help us to use it wisely. Keep us from greed. Bless those who grow food. Give wisdom to those who transport it. And give insight to those who are attempting to increase resources through research, development, conservation and political action.*

MONDAY 30 SEPTEMBER
SYMBOL AND REALITY

READING MARK 8:11–21
'"Why does this generation ask for a miraculous sign? . . . When I broke the five loaves for the five thousand, how many basketfuls of pieces did you pick up?" "Twelve," they replied. "And when I broke the seven loaves for the four thousand, how many basketfuls of pieces did you pick up?" They answered, "Seven"' (vv. 12b,19,20, NIV).

THE DISCIPLES' LACK of understanding is emphasised more and more as Mark's story progresses. How they could be worried about bread after two miraculous feedings is almost beyond belief. Mark uses their incredibly shallow response to stir his readers to deeper understanding. But it doesn't just come to us on a plate. Understanding has to be sought. To achieve it we need to appreciate the symbolic value placed on numbers by Mark and his generation.

Five and twelve, the numbers associated with the first miracle, were important to Jews; five books of the Law, twelve tribes of Israel. Four and seven were Gentile numbers, reminding Mark's generation of the four corners of the earth and the seven(ty) Gentile nations.

To those who have eyes to see and ears to hear, this central section of Mark outlines emphatically the universal importance of the mission of Jesus. The bulk of his preaching was in Palestine. The vast majority of his followers were Jews. But his actions symbolise the reality of his wider mission.

6:30–44
8:1–10

Jesus fed two groups of people, one in Jewish territory and one in the Gentile area of Decapolis. Jesus responded to Gentile distress, healing the Syro-Phoenician woman's daughter. He healed the deaf mute in Decapolis, which was also Gentile territory, having travelled through Sidon, a Gentile stronghold.

7:24–30

7:31–37

TO PONDER *If we follow Jesus our vision will extend far beyond our limited, immediate objectives.*

TUESDAY 1 OCTOBER
INSIGHT – I

READING MARK 8:27–33
'Peter answered, "You are the Christ"' (v. 29, NIV).

THE WATERSHED of Mark's gospel, is how one commentator has described Peter's recognition of Christ. Everything has led up to this point. The blindness of the disciples, who would not see in spite of all the indications; the obtuseness of the authorities who heard, but would not accept what they heard; the fascination of the crowds who followed the miracle-worker as though he was a travelling circus act, is all put aside. Jesus is revealed to Peter, his closest friend and most ardent disciple, as what he really is; the Messiah, the Christ, the anointed one of God. It is a great moment, which we can all share.

We have seen and heard enough in this gospel to convince us that Jesus is the Christ, Son of the living God. We can shout Hallelujah! and press on with new enthusiasm, assured that everything will be well in the end. We are being prepared, so it seems, for a happy ending.

What a disappointment, then, to see Jesus calling Peter 'Satan'. How ungrateful of him! What a shock to the first readers of the gospel! When all is set fair, we are buffeted by this unseemly outburst, and made uncomfortable again. That is the way of the gospel. That is the way of Christ. He disturbs our complacency and brings us up with a jolt. Belief is not sufficient. The sublimest insight is not enough. Insight must be followed by commitment. Not commitment to a warrior who will conquer all before him, but commitment to a cross, a path of human pain and suffering with our only consolation the consolation of knowing that Jesus trod the way before us. It is at once a picture of the greatest sorrow and the greatest joy.

TO PONDER

No matter what heights of knowledge we attain, no matter what depths of despair we may plumb, Christ has been there before us.

WEDNESDAY 2 OCTOBER
A SPIRIT OF POWER

READING MARK 8:34—9:1
'"I tell you the truth, some who are standing here will not taste death before they see the kingdom of God come with power"' (9:1, NIV).

THE KINGDOM OF GOD is a kingdom of power, the power of the Spirit which descended at Pentecost. Jesus' promise to his disciples was that some of them would live to see the kingdom come with power. Later in this volume we shall look at the record of that coming, as we contemplate the events immediately following the crucifixion and resurrection of our Lord.

Acts 1—5
WoL 2—31
Dec

But at this stage we leave Mark's story with the promise ringing in our ears; a promise which can be fulfilled in the heart of each one of us, a promise which can be fulfilled in the Church today. The power of Christ is clearly not the power of material conquest. It is not political domination or absolute control of our surroundings. It is the power to endure, to absorb the hurt of the world, and relate that hurt to a loving Father who offers us his Spirit to live and work in us.

The power of the Kingdom of God is different from power as the world sees it. It is as different as Peter's idea of the conquering Messiah was from Jesus' experience as the crucified Messiah. It is a power which can afford to be powerless, for it knows that ultimately it will be victorious, the power of God himself.

8:29 8:31

A VERSE

Power, power, power divine,
Power, power, Lord, be it mine;
Power thy promise, power my plea,
Lord, let thy power descend upon me.
  (Frederick Booth-Tucker, SASB Chorus 93)

EZEKIEL

Disaster struck Judah in 597 BC. King Nebuchadnezzar captured Jerusalem after a long siege. He deposed the king of Judah – a young man called Jehoiachin (Jeconiah) who had only reigned for three months – and carried him to exile in Babylon. Many other influential people were taken too. Nebuchadnezzar wanted to lessen Judah's power and make Judah unable to rebel against him again, yet just able to keep on functioning as a puppet kingdom under his control.

Among those deported to Babylon was a young priest, Ezekiel. We know nothing about his background in Judah. We can only guess he knew Jeremiah and was in sympathy with him. We sense the strong influence of the older man. But neither mentions the other in his writing, so we have no direct evidence of their relationship.

The book of Ezekiel is arranged in chronological order. Ezekiel describes the early years of exile when many hoped that Judah would shortly be restored. He takes us through to another disaster, eleven years after the first. Nebuchadnezzar again entered Jerusalem. This time he utterly destroyed the great city. From that point on, Ezekiel provided a lone voice of hope to the exiles in Babylon. His message became one of encouragement rather than condemnation. He offered them the prospect of showers of blessing and a new Jerusalem which would one day rise from the ashes of the old. Then, he promised, a new spirit would be placed within them, a spirit of flesh rather than stone. Almost six hundred years later his prophecy was fulfilled with the gift of the Holy Spirit at Pentecost. And the whole world changed.

THURSDAY 3 OCTOBER
THE STORM CENTRE

READING EZEKIEL 1:1–12
'Where the lightning was flashing, something shone like bronze. At the centre of the storm, I saw what looked like four living creatures in human form' (vv. 4b,5, GNB).

EZEKIEL'S VISIONS are remarkable. They are vivid, bright, exotic, full of strange creatures and indescribable mechanisms. In these days of science fiction, special effects and video presentations, we can possibly picture Ezekiel's visions more easily than earlier generations could. More images flow through our minds than they did then. We have access not only to books (to which earlier generations had rather limited access) but to glossy magazines and newspapers, photographs, films, video and computer graphics. Blindness, despite Braille, various electronic aids, and special education, is possibly a greater handicap in our visually-oriented society than ever it was.

Ezekiel's fantastic visions become more contemporary as each day passes. The ongoing centuries have obscured much of their symbolism. We no longer know all the background. But much of the meaning remains, and can be discovered through careful study of parts of his long work.

However, before we search out the voice of God in the sensational, violent, picturesque world of Ezekiel's visions, there is a little warning tucked away in today's study portion. In the midst of the flashing lightning, Ezekiel draws our attention to the centre of the storm. It is at the centre, in the eye of the storm that we find a little oasis of calm. Elijah found it when God spoke to him in a soft whisper. Ezekiel's experience was different from Elijah's, but still God is at the centre of it all.

v. 5

1 Kgs 19:12

TO PONDER *We must not let fascination with the detail of Ezekiel's visions deflect us from the central theme of his writings, the overwhelming presence of God.*

FRIDAY 4 OCTOBER
WHEELS WITHIN WHEELS

READING EZEKIEL 1:13–21
'Their appearance was . . . as it were a wheel within a wheel . . . Their rims were full of eyes round about . . . Wherever the spirit would go, they went, and the wheels rose along with them; for the spirit of the living creatures was in the wheels' (vv. (16),18b,20, RSV).

'WHEELS WITHIN WHEELS' is a phrase, perhaps not so common these days as it once was, which conveys an atmosphere of something complicated, involved and probably a little underhand. It creates a picture of unseen workings, things happening which people do not wish to bring to the light of day.

The phrase originates from Ezekiel's vision of creatures moving every which way, on wheels which intersect each other. When you try to work out the physical possibility of wheels working in this manner, the mind whirls. Such a system, it seems to me, could not work in practice, though I stand to be corrected by some with more knowledge of mechanics. [v. 16 NIV, GNB etc.]

But the physical possibility is not our main concern. Drawing pictures, or making models of Ezekiel's creatures is an interesting exercise, but not of great spiritual importance. Our concern is with the reality symbolised by the wheels. The reality is spiritual. Forces which motivated the human spirit can drive it in any direction at any moment. Such spiritual forces can be given over to the direction of God. Or they can be used by Satan. Ezekiel pictures creatures wholly given over to direction by God. They act almost like the arms and legs of God, able to go exactly where the spirit leads them without let or hindrance. They are all-seeing, all-powerful and fully open to God's will.

Ezekiel's visions seek to express the majesty, power and knowledge of God. Six centuries later, God expressed himself in the form of a single, vulnerable individual who was also fully open to his will. [TO PONDER]

SATURDAY 5 OCTOBER
NO IDOLS

READING EZEKIEL 1:22–28
'This was the appearance of the likeness of the glory of the Lord. When I saw it, I fell face down, and I heard the voice of one speaking' (v. 28b, NIV).

EZEKIEL KNOWS his vivid picture language can be misunderstood. Pictures can be interpreted many different ways. What one person finds captivating means nothing to another. Some of us appreciate colour, some of us form. Some of us want pictures to remind us closely of reality. Others find abstract art fascinating. Some marvel at intricate draughtsmanship. Others gasp at brilliant simplicity.

Ezekiel's greatest fear was that people would misunderstand his visions and think of them as actual portraits of God. He was terrified people would turn his visions into idols, and worship the vision instead of the spiritual reality behind it. Hence today's verse.

Ezekiel's clearest picture of God is still at several removes from reality. He sees not God, but the 'appearance' of God. And in case we should think that the 'appearance' of God is the real thing, he tells us that it is simply the 'appearance of the likeness'. And in case we should think that that is the real thing, he emphasises that it is not God himself he sees, but only his glory.

We can compare Ezekiel's encounter with God to Moses' experience in the desert. We remember the vision. It imprints the encounter in our memory, and makes it easy to recall. Yet the significance of the encounter is not in the vision, it is in the voice which pierces through the brightness.

TO PONDER *No matter how grand our vision, no matter how great our ambition, unless we listen to God's voice, our vision will be pointless.*

SUNDAY 6 OCTOBER
A REBELLIOUS HOUSE

READING EZEKIEL 2
'The Spirit came into me and raised me to my feet, and I heard him speaking to me . . . Whether they listen or fail to listen – for they are a rebellious house – they will know that a prophet has been among them' (vv. 2,5, NIV).

ENDURANCE is one of the prime qualities required of any prophet. Rebellion against God is difficult to quell. Our God-given human spirit of independence ensures that we do not easily accept direction from an outside source, not even from a prophet of God.

Bringing up children, educating teenagers, training potential employees, are processes which take place against resistance. The difficulty of acquiring and retaining knowledge is not all that makes education and training a painful undertaking. Much of the pain is due to our desire to do things our own way, rather than how we are taught. Often, of course, this independent spirit is positive. Without rebellion against inadequate and antiquated systems we would still be in the darkness of the middle ages. But if God is to speak to us, human barriers of resistance need to be broken down. God uses persistent prophets to overcome the barriers of our natural human spirit.

The Spirit came into Ezekiel, raised him to his feet and gave him the strength and purpose to speak out God's message to his generation. The Spirit assured Ezekiel that God was with him in spite of the people's rejection. However much people listened or failed to listen, was not Ezekiel's concern. His only concern must be to do the will of God and continue to preach, whatever the reaction to his preaching. Ezekiel's example is not a perfect pattern for us to follow, but we can learn much from his persistent refusal to allow himself to be swayed by public opinion.

PRAYER SUBJECT: *For endurance.*

PRAYER: *Father in Heaven, you speak to us through your Spirit. Help us to obey the Spirit's promptings, regardless of the cost to ourselves. Give us the power to persist in following your will, even when it means running counter to the spirit of the age in which we live.*

MONDAY 7 OCTOBER
IDENTIFICATION

READING EZEKIEL 3:1–15
'"Son of man, eat what is before you, eat this scroll; then go and speak . . ." So I ate it, and it tasted as sweet as honey in my mouth . . . and I went in bitterness and in the anger of my spirit, with the strong hand of the Lord upon me' (vv. 1,3b,14b, NIV).

v. 3b

DID EZEKIEL ENJOY the tough task that was set before him? The impression given here is that he did. He took the scroll, ate it, and it tasted as sweet as honey in his mouth. It all sounds so simple. It seems so primitive, as though the idea that 'we are what we eat' has been taken literally. But there must be more to it than that, otherwise we are looking at Ezekiel on the same level as we would look, say, at those who leave a tape recorder on while they sleep, hoping to increase their knowledge of a particular subject.

Ezekiel was being told in a striking, symbolic way, to identify completely with the message he had been called on to proclaim. He was being shown that proclaiming God's message will bring sweetness into the life of the messenger. But the initial experience of joy, elation and sweetness, was not a foretaste of what his ministry would be like. It was simply a reminder, an initial assurance that the road he was taking was the right one.

v. 7

As soon as he has eaten, bitterness returns. He is again told his task will be hard. And the Lord tells him he will make him hard enough to resist the fierce words of those bound to oppose him. His terror is not lessened by the sweet-tasting scroll, but the memory of that sweetness will sustain him in spite of his terror.

Still in shock, Ezekiel comes to the Exiles close to Babylon and sits amongst them, unable to speak for a week. When his voice returns, the message he proclaims is a simple one, so simple we might almost take it for granted – a message of responsibility.

TUESDAY 8 OCTOBER
THE WATCHMAN

READING EZEKIEL 3:16–21 (also 33:1–9)
'Son of man, I have made you a watchman for the house of Israel; so hear the word I speak and give them warning from me' (v. 17, NIV).

RESPONSIBILITY, claimed mathematician Charles Coulson, is what marks out a man from a machine. He said, nearly thirty years ago, 'There is no difficulty, in principle, in designing a machine that will invent new things, that will learn by its own mistakes, that will even be able to reproduce itself. But no one has suggested that we can design a machine that will consciously exercise responsibility . . . thinking about responsibility is ultimately thinking about what makes us really and truly human.'

Ezekiel would agree with Coulson. Over and over again, sometimes one way, sometimes another, Ezekiel emphasises the supreme importance of human responsibility. Jeremiah before him had said that an old proverb 'The fathers have eaten sour grapes, and the children's teeth are set on edge' would no longer apply. Up to that time people had taken refuge in thinking that their own misfortune, their own misdeeds were somehow related to the misdeeds of their ancestors. 'Instead, (says Jeremiah) everyone will die for his own sin; whoever eats sour grapes – his own teeth will be set on edge'. Jer 31:29

Jer 31:30

Ezekiel, too, quotes this proverb but not until he has made it clear that responsibility means more than just taking care of one's own skin. The 'I'm-all-right-Jack-who-cares-about-you?' type of philosophy has no place in Ezekiel's thinking. 18:2

Ezekiel stresses the role of the watchman. His task is to warn of impending danger. If he doesn't, he becomes responsible, not just for his own fate, but also for the fate of his friends. A message repeated in ch. 33.

True individual responsibility includes responsibility for others. TO PONDER

WEDNESDAY 9 OCTOBER
MASTERING PRINCIPLES

READING EZEKIEL 4:1–4,10–16
'I replied, "No, Sovereign Lord! I have never defiled myself. From childhood on I have never eaten meat from any animal that died a natural death or was killed by wild animals. I have never eaten any food considered unclean"' (v. 14, GNB).

EZEKIEL WAS IN IRAQ, a captive Jew. The Iraqis (they were called *Babylonians at that time) had conquered Jerusalem, but conquest had not satisfied them. Jerusalem was now under threat of complete destruction.

Ezekiel knew this. The Lord had told him so. Whether directly in a vision or through reliable informants does not matter. The important thing is, Ezekiel knew it was a word from the Lord.

However, Ezekiel was not just told to convey the message of impending destruction to his fellow exiles, he was asked to act out the siege that was going to take place. We could hardly imagine anything more likely to inflame the situation. In those days people believed that acting out the siege was almost the same as causing it to happen. By predicting the destruction, Ezekiel had to risk people thinking he had caused the destruction.

Acts 10:14   Ezekiel was told to show the people the horror of the situation by eating 'unclean' food, cooked on human excrement. His protest against this reminds us of the protest of Peter, centuries later. To get his unpalatable message across, Ezekiel had to overcome an overwhelming distaste of what he was being asked to do. He had to risk misunderstanding and the possibility of being thought a traitor.

TO PONDER   *When everyone conforms, it takes a brave man to resist. When everyone calls for resistance, it takes a brave man to overcome his distaste of the enemy, and to proclaim that resistance is wrong.*

*Babylon, the capital of ancient Babylonia was about 50 miles southwest of modern Baghdad.

THURSDAY 10 OCTOBER
THIS IS THE END . . .

READING EZEKIEL 7:2–4, (5–9); 6:8,9a
'"Mortal man," he said, "this is what I, the Sovereign Lord, am saying to the land of Israel: This is the end for the whole land!"' (7:2, GNB).
'"I will let some escape the slaughter and be scattered among the nations, where they will live in exile"' (6:8,9a, GNB).

. . . BUT NOT QUITE! Ezekiel's words are stern, unbending and fierce. Again and again he thunders out the message, Israel is doomed. In ch. 7 he wants to emphasise doom so much that he repeats the same words in succeeding passages.

7:2–4 = 7:5–9

Sometimes the voice of hope seems to be drowned out completely. But by looking backwards as well as forwards in the book we discover little verses which dispel despair. Referring back to chapter 6 we discover that destruction won't be absolute. Always there will be a remnant.

Like Elijah, Amos, Isaiah and others before him Ezekiel sees hope for the future despite the blackness of present and past. Perhaps it is easier to hope in times of great crisis, for during disturbance, conflict and trouble there is always the possibility of real change occurring. In times of peace and tranquillity, though the majority of the population may be content to plod their placid way through life, the poor and dispossessed will be unable to see any real prospect of change in their condition.

1 Kgs 19:18
Amos 9:13ff.
Micah 4:6,7
Isa 6:13 etc.

Swift to its close ebbs out life's little day;
Earth's joys grow dim, its glories pass away;
Change and decay in all around I see;
O thou who changest not, abide with me!
(Henry Francis Lyte, SASB 670.)

A VERSE

The more we understand that God does not change, the more we realise that we have to change. Times of crisis, though unpleasant, help to make this clear.

TO PONDER

FRIDAY 11 OCTOBER
INSIGHT – II

READING EZEKIEL 8:1–4, 7–13
'The Spirit lifted me up between earth and heaven, and brought me in visions of God to Jerusalem... "Son of man, have you seen what the elders of the house of Israel are doing in the dark, every man in his room of pictures? For they say, 'The Lord does not see us, the Lord has forsaken the land'"' (vv. 3b,12, RSV)

THE SCENE SWITCHES from Babylon to Jerusalem. Ezekiel's vision is projected into the temple. The way *RSV* expresses, it, we could almost think Ezekiel is describing men furtively watching video nasties, 'each man in his room of pictures'. That's not, of course, the case but a similar tendency is at work. At times of change many reject consistent moral values. People try mixtures of old pagan ritual and new amoral 'freedoms'. They don't realise they'll lose their self control, trapped by forces beyond their command.

The elders of Judah felt God had rejected them, so they turned to the old ways of their ancestors. They indulged in ancient rituals with a strong, sexual element. Their pictures were fertility idols. Their worship involved sexual acts. They believed such actions would make them and the land fertile. We commented earlier on similar ideas related to Ezekiel's actions. He built siege works round a model Jerusalem. People would consider his action had helped to bring about Jerusalem's downfall.

4:1–12,
WoL 9 Oct

The Spirit gave Ezekiel insight into what was going on. He knew his people were turning in despair to gods that were not gods. And he knew the chief offenders were society's leaders, those who formed opinion and directed the temple information machine. Even a member of a most influential and trustworthy family, Jaazaniah son of Shaphan, was caught up in the attempt to return to occult practices and their pagan roots.

6:9 8:6 14:3

v. 11, see Jer
26:24 29:3
36:12 &
2 Kgs
22:8–14

TO PONDER *Insight must be followed by commitment. Ezekiel committed himself to share his vision with others, and to encourage them to remain faithful to God.*

SATURDAY 12 OCTOBER
NO PROPS

READING EZEKIEL 12:1–16
'They have eyes to see but do not see and ears to hear but do not hear . . . I have made you a sign to the house of Israel . . . They will know that I am the Lord, when I disperse them among the nations' (from vv. 2,6,15, NIV).

JESUS USED PHRASES and ideas from Ezekiel. One favourite phrase concerns seeing and not seeing, hearing and not hearing. Its meaning is clearer in Ezekiel than it seems to be in Mark. In Ezekiel exile has already occurred. Ezekiel is prophesying to a people who are already in exile. Clearly, the people have seen what is happening, and are still blind, they have heard what has occurred, and are still deaf.

Mark 4:9–12

Mark 4:30–32 cf. Ezek 17:23

See intro

Some scholars suggest, because of this chapter, that Ezekiel was really in Jerusalem, rather than seeing a vision of what was happening there. But we need not resort to such drastic measures to make sense of Ezekiel's actions. In exile the people were now relatively secure. Ezekiel apart, they had no idea how bad and corrupt things were back at home. They knew a king of sorts still reigned in Jerusalem. The city had not been destroyed. They could still regard it as their spiritual home. They could still rely, so they thought, on the bricks and mortar, the ritual and music, the sacrifice and offerings which took place there. The material props of their religion were still in existence, even though they were hundreds of miles away from them.

Ezekiel's actions told them their sense of security was false. The last props of their religion were going to be taken away. The 'king' would be brought to them in Exile, blinded by his captors. The land would be stripped bare.

2 Kgs 25:7

v. 13

All the props of religion were taken away from the exiles. Yet in exile Judaism became strong, and from exile revival returned to Israel.

TO PONDER

SUNDAY 13 OCTOBER
PARABLE AND ALLEGORY

READING EZEKIEL 17 (1–10,22–24)
'Birds of every kind will nest in it; they will find shelter in the shade of its branches. All the trees of the field will know that I the Lord bring down the tall tree and make the low tree grow tall. I dry up the green tree and make the dry tree flourish' (vv. 23b,24, NIV).

COMPARED TO JESUS' PARABLES the picture story in this chapter is complicated, even contrived. It must have been clear to the people who originally heard it, but three slightly different explanations surface in the written record (vv. 11–15,16–18,22–24). Probably Ezekiel's words were noted down, then developed by Ezekiel himself, or by his disciples. As conditions changed, the original meaning became less clear. Different interpretations of the eagles and the vine arose. The final interpretation is what we concentrate on today.

Once more we find allusions to Ezekiel's picture in the gospels. Jesus spoke of the mustard seed becoming a great tree in whose shade the birds will come and make their nests (Mark 4:30–32). The implication is clear. The people of Israel, whether in exile or back in Israel's God. Like an enormous tree which plays host not only to the local, very visible eagles, but also to birds of every kind from near and far, Israel's God will welcome others under his sheltering branches.

For all his concentration on the needs of the people of Israel, Ezekiel's vision is a wide one. He sees that God will raise up unknown peoples to become great, and that the mighty, powerful peoples of his day will be the small and insignificant peoples of tomorrow.

PRAYER SUBJECT: *For powerful rulers.*

PRAYER: *Lord, help all who have power over people, to remember that they do not have absolute control. You alone know the reason for their actions. You alone know the consequences of their actions. You alone know the final outcome. Remind them, their power is temporary. Help them to exercise it with the welfare of others in mind, including the welfare of future generations.*

MONDAY 14 OCTOBER
RESPONSIBILITY

READING EZEKIEL 18:1–9,25–32
'Behold, all souls are mine . . . the soul that sins shall die. If a man is righteous and does what is lawful and right . . . he is righteous, he shall surely live, says the Lord God' (vv. 4,5a,9b, RSV).

INDIVIDUAL responsibility was not a new idea in Ezekiel's day. It's there in the Ten Commandments. It is implied by the way God deals with individuals throughout the Old Testament. But equally a nagging thought remains that 'visiting the iniquity of the fathers upon the children to the third and fourth generation', might somehow outweigh the need to be careful about one's own actions.

Exod 20: 1–17
Deut 5:7–21

Exod 20:5
Deut 6:9

The idea of sins being visited on future generations is meant to be a warning to us, here and now, to take care. Our sins will affect following generations. But how easily a warning becomes an excuse. Instead of taking the warning and thinking, 'I must not fail for my children's sake' we find an excuse to say 'My failure is my forebears' fault.'

Looking at our world today we see good reasons to think like that. How can we unravel the hurt of war previous generations left? How can we live at peace with those who killed our fathers, mothers, even our brothers, sisters and cousins? Aren't their sins visited on us, leaving a trail of bitterness and recrimination which fate decrees that we follow?

No, says Ezekiel. Look to your own actions. Forget past failures. They need not weigh you down. Think of present and future. They are not decreed by fate, but created by your actions. If you are righteous, you will live. If you sin, you will die. Such statements are true – against a back cloth of eternity.

Individual responsibility means we are no longer at the mercy of blind fate, for we can 'get ourselves a new heart and a new spirit'. TO PONDER

TUESDAY 15 OCTOBER
A SERMON

READING EZEKIEL 20:1–12
'In the seventh year, in the fifth month on the tenth day, some of the elders of Israel came to enquire of the Lord, and they sat down in front of me' (v. 1, NIV).

THE FREEDOM ENJOYED by Ezekiel and his fellow Jews in captivity is remarkable. Good communications existed between Babylon and Judah. Without them, Babylon could not have retained control of Judah. But beyond the official contacts, needed for orderly management of an empire, there seem to have been good personal communications. Of course, several groups of exiles came, as we know from the Biblical account. Possibly some were brought to Babylon at other times as well. But however it occurred, Ezekiel knew what was going on in Judah, and Jeremiah at the other end knew what was happening in Babylon. No record remains of direct communication between them, but similarities of approach lead us to think Ezekiel was possibly a disciple of Jeremiah during his early years in Jerusalem.

606 BC?
597BC
586BC
582BC

8:6

Jer 24 &
Jer 29

Babylonian records of Jewish business transactions show that Jewish commercial life prospered in Babylon. Jehoiachin, the true king of Judah who lived 37 years in Babylonian exile gained more and more status, and it has been suggested Babylon was grooming him for return to Judah to take up his kingdom again. What went wrong to stop that, we can only guess.

2 Kgs
25:27–30

Jewish religious life continued too. There was no bar on Ezekiel telling the whole story of Hebrew religion. The sermon in ch. 20 retells in classic style the story of the Exodus and the history of the Hebrews, like Stephen's speech and other accounts. A typical synagogue sermon.

Acts 7
13:16–39
Psalm 78
Neh 9:6–31

TO PONDER *Listening to Ezekiel retelling their traditions, enabled the exiles to live upright lives separated from their traditional roots.*

WEDNESDAY 16 OCTOBER
A SECOND EXODUS

READING EZEKIEL 20:32–44
'I will bring you into the desert of the nations and there, face to face, I will execute judgment upon you . . . You will know that I am the Lord, when I deal with you for my name's sake and not according to your evil ways' (vv. 35,44a, NIV).

MOSES LED THE PEOPLE on the Exodus through the desert. It was a glorious chapter in the history of Israel, a focus for later generations, a period of greatness to which they look back with nostalgia. It was the record of a great salvation. Yet during the Exodus, throughout the time that they were being saved, the people rebelled, unable to accept the discomfort of desert life as a preparation for the promised land beyond.

Exod 13:18

Exod 16:2
32:1,2 etc.

It is ever thus. Great crises may unite us for a time, but when the initial crisis passes the discomfort is felt and discontent surfaces.

Ezekiel had no illusions about the second Exodus. God was bringing his people out into the desert of the nations – into Babylon, and all its surrounding areas – in order to judge them for their past wickedness. God will judge them face to face, not through Moses, nor even through Ezekiel, but directly. They will have access to him themselves. It is an awesome prospect. No one could survive such a judgement, except that the Lord will not judge according to what the people deserve, but in order to save his name and reputation. Ezekiel is grasping after a doctrine of salvation which comes close to New Testament thinking. He knows that none of us can stand before God's judgement. All we can do is to rely on God's mercy.

v. 35

v. 35

Hosea, long before Ezekiel, perhaps came closer to New Testament thinking, but our study of the latter parts of Ezekiel will bring us into areas which enabled New Testament ideas to be understood.

TO PONDER

Hos 11:1,9
14:1 etc.

THURSDAY 17 OCTOBER
BEYOND WEEPING

READING EZEKIEL 24:15–27
'Do not lament or weep or shed any tears. Groan quietly; do not mourn for the dead' (vv. 16b,17a, NIV).
'You will not mourn or weep but will waste away because of your sins and groan among yourselves. Ezekiel will be a sign to you' (vv. 23b,24a, NIV).

SOME SITUATIONS are so grave, nothing can express our anguish. In the face of disaster there may be screaming and shrieking. But then, numbness, shock and a sense of unreality. Some emotional pain is so far beyond endurance that no reaction is appropriate. No response can be made.

When Ezekiel's wife died it was a severe blow to him. 'The delight of his eyes' was taken away. Normal reaction was to weep, to express sorrow and so enable grief to turn to healing. But the situation was too serious for that. Ezekiel's own pain was to be mirrored ten thousand times over by the catastrophe about to befall Jerusalem. It was going to be destroyed. Such destruction was beyond the normal process of grieving.

Today's passage is the only one where Ezekiel's name is used. Elsewhere he is addressed as 'Son of man', representative of the human race, God's special envoy to the people. But the blanket description 'Son of man' will not do for today's crisis. Today it is Ezekiel, the man himself, who is the sign. His personal reaction will affect the rest of the population. They will all be struck dumb by the hand of God. Ezekiel's silence and shock will be a stronger sign than his silver speech. His sweet songs might fall on deaf ears, but his deathly silence will cut them to the heart.

A PRAYER *The deepest suffering is silent. Let us pray that chatter and cheer will return to the stricken places of the earth in these days. May the silence of famine, defeat and fear be driven from our planet by a spirit of joyous communication.*

FRIDAY 18 OCTOBER
REPENTANCE

READING EZEKIEL 33:10,11
'"Son of man, say to the house of Israel, 'This is what you are saying; "Our offences and sins weigh us down, and we are wasting away because of them. How then can we live?"' Say to them, 'As surely as I live, declares the Sovereign Lord, I take no pleasure in the death of the wicked, but rather that they turn from their ways and live. Turn! Turn from your evil ways! Why will you die, O house of Israel?'"' (vv. 10,11, NIV).

THE CENTRAL PIVOT of Ezekiel's prophecy is in today's passage, full of plain teaching which we can meditate on at length. So today's reading and comment is shorter than most, and the quoted passage longer.

Ezekiel's clarity and legalistic tone sometimes lead scholars to claim he over-simplifies problems of evil, goodness and judgement. He seems to connect evil and death too directly. But we have seen how he accounts for the death of the innocent in his complicated statement of the watchman's responsibility. We must also consider that Ezekiel is starting to realise the possibility of eternal life beyond the grave.

3:16–21

Ch. 37
WoL 23 Oct

Judgement is more than survival or a sentence of death on earth. Judgement belongs to the next world, too. Ezekiel's simple, legalistic terminology only makes full sense when related to a final judgement day. Our responsibility is to turn from our evil ways, look to God, and trust him for mercy on that day.

> *O turn, sinners, turn ye, for why will ye die?*
> *'Tis Jesus, your Saviour, is asking you why;*
> *And now he is waiting his pardon to give,*
> *O turn, sinners, turn unto Jesus and live!*
>   *(Benjamin Wilks,* SASB 1953 ed. 275)*

A VERSE

* An early-day salvationist, a converted drunkard who wrote these simple words to the tune of one of his old drinking songs.

SATURDAY 19 OCTOBER
SWEET WORDS

READING EZEKIEL 33:21,22,30—33
'You are to them like one who sings love songs with a beautiful voice and plays well on an instrument, for they hear what you say, but they will not do it' (v. 32, RSV).

INSINCERE LOVE SONGS are not new. In Ezekiel's time there were already people who entertained others by singing love songs. It was hardly the industry it has become today, but people made a good living from acting out what others felt, and putting it into words.

Ezekiel's message was not popular. Like Jeremiah, he advocated submission to Babylon. He asked for holiness and justice. He advocated self denial and responsibility towards the whole community. But the way he put his message over was attractive and interesting. His actions kept the audience entranced. His words sounded like music in their ears. Sometimes Ezekiel was struck dumb but that seems only to have increased the entertainment value.

3:26

He gained a reputation. People came to watch and to listen. His audience grew — but it was just that, an audience rather than a congregation. They were not bound together by a common allegiance to the word of God. They were simply concert-goers, swayed by the mood of the moment, making no lasting commitment.

If Ezekiel had asked, they would probably have given in an offering. They might even have pledged their support, and made great gestures of solidarity with him. But to go away and alter their own life-style? No. That would be too much to ask.

TO PONDER *Giving a popular format to unpopular messages may be a temporary help. Lasting changes can only come about with a change of heart, and long-term, sacrificial commitments. Pop concerts are no substitute for commitment to a change of life-style.*

SUNDAY 20 OCTOBER
THE GOOD SHEPHERD

READING EZEKIEL 34:1–16
'As a shepherd seeks out his flock . . . so will I seek out my sheep . . . I will seek the lost, and I will bring back the strayed, and I will bind up the crippled, and I will strengthen the weak, and the fat and the strong I will watch over; I will feed them in justice' (vv. 12a,16, RSV).

HOW COMFORTING! A fine preview of the New Testament good shepherd (John 10). The parallel is plain to all, but look carefully at 'watching over' the fat and the strong. The shepherd is suspicious of the fat and the strong! How have they become strong? How has their prosperity come about? Has the fat sheep taken more than his share of nourishment, and pushed his weaker brother out? Does he need watching to ensure he doesn't keep on doing it?

Yes, indeed, as other versions of v. 16 make clear. They use the Hebrew, rather than the old Greek text used in this instance by *RSV*. *KJV* has 'I will destroy the fat and the strong,' *NIV* 'The sleek and the strong I will destroy'. *LB* adds a different slant on feeding, 'I will feed them, yes – feed them punishment!' Comforting words have a sting in the tail. In the terms of yesterday's comment, throwing pounds, marks, dollars or yen at a problem while influenced by a pop concert may placate a conscience or two. It will make no long-term difference. Givers will remain rich, recipients poor; for proper long-term care of the weak would mean real pain and sacrifice for the strong, and that is unacceptable except to a small minority amongst whom are numbered earnest Christians of all kinds.

Jesus tells of a shepherd who left the ninety and nine to look after themselves, and sought the lost one (Matt 18:12 Luke 15:4) over whom he rejoiced. This message is very close to that of Ezekiel. Both demand real priority for the weak, if anything like justice is to be done. This week's prayer subject shows the other side of the coin of last week's.

PRAYER SUBJECT: *For weak citizens.*

PRAYER: *Lord, help all those who are weak – and help those of us who are strong not to complain when you do. Help us to work with you to achieve justice, even when it hurts us personally.*

MONDAY 21 OCTOBER
YOU ARE PEOPLE

READING EZEKIEL 34:20–31
'I myself will judge . . . I will send down showers in season; there will be showers of blessing . . . You my sheep, the sheep of my pasture, are people, and I am your God, declares the Sovereign Lord' (from vv. 20,26,31, NIV).

THE BEAUTIFUL WORDS of this section conjure up an idyllic picture in our mind; a picture of prosperity, peace and plenty, the like of which has rarely been enjoyed until our present century.

Even in prosperous areas of the 'West' we have had sharp reminders in recent years that prosperity and plenty are not guaranteed, despite all the sophisticated resouces at our disposal. Drought in the USA and continental Europe has brought some farmers to their knees. Water shortages, though causing discomfort rather than real hardship, have made us slightly more aware of the importance of water, and we take it a little less for granted than we did. Even we British, grousing and griping about our climate, have sometimes longed for showers to revive parched ground and cool our over-heated bodies.

Ezekiel's vivid picture of blessing is almost entirely material in outlook. Abundant crops, plentiful water, shelter, security from thieves and so on.

v. 31 Two points, though, stand out above the others. Firstly, people are people. They are not sheep, whose needs are simply material. People need more than material security in order to enjoy showers of blessing. Secondly people
vv. 20,22 need justice. It is not sufficient to be rich, powerful, materially at ease with oneself, while others go hungry, and remain powerless. Being human involves responsi-
v. 31 bility – responding to the needs of others.

TO PONDER *The 'I'm-all-right-Jack' type of philosophy is not simply*
WoL 8 Oct *inadequate, it is sub-human.*

TUESDAY 22 OCTOBER
A NEW HEART

READING EZEKIEL 36:22–28
'I will give you a new heart and put a new spirit in you; I will remove from you your heart of stone and give you a heart of flesh' (v. 26, NIV).

REPENTANCE IS the central pivot of Ezekiel's message. Today's passage shows how to achieve it. Repentance is possible, for God offers us the possibility of a change of heart. 'The leopard cannot change his spots' but the Christian is a continual witness to the possibility of a change of heart. 33:10,11

Ezekiel did not know Christ, but he knew the Christian's God. He received inspiration from God through visions, reading, and contact with Jeremiah and others. As he wrestled with the problems of his people's continuing faithlessness, he saw that their only chance was a God-given revolution in attitude. Repentance, renewal, renovation, restoration, regeneration, reform, resurgence, resurrection and a dozen other revival words, I'm sure, would apply to the thoughts racing through his consciousness. And he saw that none of these things could happen without a change of heart.

Ezekiel would not have been puzzled when Jesus said 'You must be born again'. He had already worked that out. Nothing less than a complete change is needed if God's blessings are to be channelled effectively towards his people. And Ezekiel makes clear that a change of heart has social implications as well as individual ones. Society has an attitude, a heart, a spirit – despite recent scorn poured upon such statements. Ezekiel notes that God's promise of a new heart is not just to individuals – though that is of over-riding importance – but to a people. John 3:7

v. 28

Individual responsibility means we are no longer at the mercy of blind fate, for we can 'get ourselves a new heart and a new spirit'. True individual responsibility includes responsibility for others. TO PONDER

WoL 14 Oct
8 Oct

WEDNESDAY 23 OCTOBER
DRY BONES

READING EZEKIEL 37:1-10
'He asked me, "Son of Man, can these bones live?" I said, "O Sovereign Lord, you alone know"... "Hear the word of the Lord!... I will make breath enter you, and you will come to life"' (vv. 3,4b,5, NIV).

RENEWAL IS POSSIBLE. Ezekiel was faced with disaster at every turn. Judah had been destroyed. Jerusalem was burnt. Valleys full of skeletons would be a common sight. Despair was everywhere. How could new life be brought into such a desperate situation? Or rather, could new life be brought into such a situation at all? His feelings must have been, on a small scale, like those who survived the holocaust. Surely life could never be the same again.

Of course, life cannot be the same again – but it can be life. And life on a greater and grander scale than was ever thought possible before. For we know the truth of resurrection. Hopes may be dashed, but hope itself can never be destroyed. Men may be executed, but man cannot thereby be extinguished. Men may be imprisoned, tortured, reduced to wrecks, but the human spirit cannot be snuffed out. Dry bones can live. The cross is the supreme example, but there are many others, too, one of which was the resurgence of the people of Judah during and after the exile.

Jer 29:5–7 Judah was destroyed. But the people of Judah lived on. They built houses, planted gardens and looked to the welfare of Babylon, as per the instructions of Jeremiah. They listened to Ezekiel, and studied their ancient laws. They kept their religion alive, though all the props of temple, liturgy, sacrifice and pilgrimage had been pulled from under them.

TO PONDER *Ezekiel's spiritual insights brought the Exiles in Babylon closer to God than ever they had been while relying on the Temple back in Jerusalem. The vision of the dry bones inspired a spiritual resurrection of the people.*

THURSDAY 24 OCTOBER
EXCLUSIVE?

READING EZEKIEL 47:21–23; 48:35
'In whatever tribe the alien settles, there you are to give him his inheritance... And the name of the city from that time on will be: "THE LORD IS THERE"' (47:23, 48:35, NIV).

ISRAEL, AFTER EZEKIEL, became a new people. They also became an exclusive people. As they settled in their land they pushed the foreigner out. They made sure that others had no say in running the Temple. They emphasised rules of purity which only the strongest adherent of Judaism could hope to maintain. They encircled the city with walls. They stopped foreigners worshipping. In short, they cut themselves off from the outside world.

Neh 13:1,4,8
Neh 10:28
13:30
Neh 7:1 etc.

In other words, they took hold of parts of Ezekiel's message, but ignored its spirit. They dreamed of an idealised Judah, with Jerusalem at its centre, as envisaged in the highly stylised chapters at the end of Ezekiel's prophecy. And they tried to bring it about by denying others access to it, quite contrary to the prophet's intention.

Ezek 40–48

It is a common temptation. We see our way of life threatened and try to preserve it by building defences round ourselves, putting up barriers and denying access to others. But Ezekiel's way, and the way of Christ, is to give access to all. The foreigner has as much right as the native-born Jew, or Englishman, American or German, Indian or Japanese – and so we could go on. In New Testament terms, the prodigal has as much right as the elder brother, a very difficult idea to take on board.

Luke 15:11–32

Christ's Church is not an exclusive body. It is an ark into which all may come with an equal right. It should offer rescue from the flood of evil, and prepare us to confront the evil which remains. Then the Lord will indeed be there.

TO PONDER

48:35

FRIDAY 25 OCTOBER
PETER (AND SILAS)–1

READING 1 PETER 1:1,2,; 5:12
'Peter, an apostle of Jesus Christ, To God's elect, strangers in the world . . . Grace and peace be yours in abundance' (vv. 1a,2b, NIV).

PETER, ABOVE ALL people, knew the power of God's grace. If anyone should have been excluded from the Church it was Peter. When Jesus was facing a crisis where he needed all the support he could get, Peter played the part of Satan. Peter tempted his Lord to reject the path of suffering and take the easy road to perdition. When Jesus was facing the cross, it was Peter who denied him. After the resurrection it was Peter who, when given his commission by Jesus, hesitated to respond because of his jealousy of another disciple. Even after Pentecost, Peter was by no means perfect. He hesitated and faltered in the face of opposition.

Mark 7:32

Mark 14:67,68
John 21:20,21
Acts 10
Gal 2:11–13

Yet it was also Peter who was filled with the Spirit and given power to galvanise the Church to action. Peter made the Church into a movement which turned the world upside down. So when Peter writes about the grace of God he knows what he is talking about. Only the power of God's grace was able to change Peter from a weak, wilful character into a spiritual leader of the people, who could inspire with both the spoken and the written word.

Acts 2:14ff.
10:10:47 etc.

Some, of course, doubt whether Peter himself wrote this letter. The Greek in which it is written is, so people say, too good for a Galilean peasant fisherman like Peter. But with the help of Silas, Paul's friend, an educated man, who probably did the writing for him, Peter's Greek would surely be as good as the next man's.

5:12

TO PONDER *Peter's letter, inspired by the Spirit, is a wonderful example of the power of God's grace, combined with the effective use of human resources. Silas, too, had his part to play.*

SATURDAY 26 OCTOBER
SUFFERING

READING 1 PETER 1:3–6
'By his great mercy we have been born anew to a living hope through the resurrection of Jesus Christ from the dead . . . In this you rejoice, though now for a little while you may have to suffer various trials' (vv. 3,6, RSV).

PIE IN THE SKY WHEN YOU DIE is an accusation often levelled at Christianity. Suffering here on earth is balanced by the hope of a new life beyond the grave. So, some argue, Christians have little incentive to make the kind of efforts needed to conquer the pain and misery of this world. Endure now, enjoy later is an open ticket to exploitation by the unscrupulous, who can so easily gain influence in, or even hi-jack the organisation of the Church.

It is a real danger. It is met by stressing Jesus' exhortations to feed the hungry, clothe the naked and look after the stranger. No Christian has the right to cause another suffering or accept suffering imposed by another in the belief that suffering in this world is trivial compared to joy in the next world. There is no piety in suffering for its own sake. There is no piety in inflicting suffering on others. Yet suffering is redemptive.

Matt 25:36,40

C. S. Lewis wrote about suffering and pain. Writing is one thing, enduring is another. A powerful drama, 'Shadowlands' tells the story of Lewis's struggle to cope with his own suffering, and more particularly, that of his wife. After seeing the play a critic wrote, 'Suffering is just about the only tool God has to enter our world and puncture our complacency'. God uses that tool, not by inflicting suffering on us, but by enduring it with us. Christ offers to a complacent world a God who suffers with us, and redeems us by taking our suffering on himself.

The God who suffers with us here in this world is indeed the one who offers us hope there in the next world. TO PONDER

SUNDAY 27 OCTOBER
SALVATION AND JOY

READING 1 PETER 1:7–9
'You believe in him and are filled with an inexpressible and glorious joy, for you are receiving the goal of your faith, the salvation of your souls' (vv. 8b,9, NIV).

A MISERABLE CHRISTIAN is almost a contradiction in terms. Some, of course, bubble over with joy more than others. Some wear joy on their faces like a badge. You can tell that they are full of glorious joy from morning to night. Others may have a serenity which is possibly even more compelling than a bubbly joy. But most of us are plain, ordinary people who have ups and downs like all the rest. Sometimes we succeed, and sometimes fail. Sometimes we laugh, sometimes weep, but mostly we go on steadily between the two extremes.

It is to the ordinary ones that Peter is speaking today. He is speaking to people, like us, who have not seen Christ in the flesh. He is speaking to people, like us, who need to be continually convinced that they really are receiving the goal of their faith, that is salvation. He is speaking to people who could easily fall away from their Christian hope.

In Peter's day, Sunday could not be set aside for worship, rest and recreation. It had to be a day like all the others. Christians met together early in the morning, to pray and to praise. They had to fit the religious part of their Christian activity in before the hurly-burly of a working day. So it was important to remind themselves every day of their vital hope. As we enjoy the benefits of a Christian Sunday of worship, prayer and praise, or as we go out to work in today's increasingly pagan society, let us use today's verses to remind ourselves the whole week through that we need not fall away from our Christian hope, whatever the pagan pressures that surround us.

PRAYER SUBJECT: *For the assurance of salvation.*

PRAYER: *Lord, come to us and reassure us of the fact of your salvation. Help us to remember at all times that we are redeemed fully by the blood of Christ Jesus our Lord.*

MONDAY 28 OCTOBER
THE SPIRIT WITHIN

READING 1 PETER 1:10–12
'This salvation was something the prophets did not fully understand ... They wondered what the Spirit of Christ within them was talking about ... even the angels in heaven would give a great deal to know more about it' (vv. 10a,11a,12b, LB).

THE WORKING OF THE SPIRIT is not easy to understand. We know about the Spirit coming at Pentecost in a new way, but what of the Old Testament? And how does the Old Testament relate to our experience today?

For Peter these were very real questions. He lived in an age not far from the Old Testament. The Old Testament was his scripture, and he turned to it for inspiration. We, too, value the Old Testament witness. We would not have undertaken so much study of Ezekiel, nor would we be looking at Zechariah in a few days time if we did not. We see them as speaking very much to their own time. The value of their words today is in the insights which they give to the way God works with his people, and the way his people react on a day to day basis. They tell us things about our reactions, and illustrate the way that God can break through to us – as well as showing up the barriers we place between ourselves and God.

But for Peter the value of the prophets was almost entirely as pointers to the future. He saw them as struggling to understand the words which the Spirit had put into their mouths. He saw them undertaking a ministry, as it were, in the dark. Perhaps we should ask ourselves if we have returned to the Old Testament condition, as Peter understood it, lacking understanding and groping in the dark. Or are we truly living in the light of the gospel?

The Church is bound to be dark, unless the light of the gospel shines through to me, and I allow the Spirit to illumine my life. TO PONDER

TUESDAY 29 OCTOBER
BE HOLY

READING 1 PETER 1:13–19
'Just as he who called you is holy, so be holy in all you do; for it is written: "Be holy, because I am holy"' (v. 15, NIV).

CHRISTIANITY is a matter of relationship, rather than one of authority. God does not simply say to us 'Do what I say, because I say so.' Instead he calls us into relationship with him and asks us to be holy, because he is holy. He identified with us by sending his Son to die for us. In turn, he asks us to identify with him completely, and commit ourselves to him.

v. 19

Being holy is a matter of relationship, not in mindless fashion, but with careful thought. Peter calls on his readers to prepare their minds. Reasoned argument is no substitute for a close relationship with God – but close relationship does not rule out argument. We use our minds as well as our emotions in this commitment to our Lord. We react to him. We question him. We entreat him. We may even, like the prophets of old, argue with him. But whatever else we do, being holy means committing ourselves to him alone.

v. 13

Tim Lenton writes 'If commitment is not first and only to God, it is worse than useless. Indeed, a commitment to something else – *even if it is something closely associated to God* – is a block and a substitute. It is not only traditionalists who fall prey to it. We can be equally wrongly committed to, say, using guitars in worship, to much speaking in tongues, to dance or drama. It is not a question of old and new, tradition and innovations. It is not, as many churchmen seem to think, a question of adding or taking away, and so losing the essence of worship. It is a question of idolatry. If we commit ourselves to anything less than God, we are not nearly there. We are very, very far away.'

A PRAYER *Lord, keep us close to you in every way. Keep our spirits sensitive to your leading, and our minds alert to your demands.*

WEDNESDAY 30 OCTOBER
PRACTICAL HOLINESS

READING 1 PETER 1:20–25
'Your faith and hope are in God' (v. 21b, RSV).
'Having purified your souls . . . love one another earnestly from the heart' (v. 22, RSV).

SOME SCHOLARS THINK 1 Peter contains extracts from a baptismal sermon. If so, the baptism could well have taken place right here. Peter says 'Your faith and hope are in God.' The candidates are then fully immersed. Peter continues 'Having purified your souls . . . love one another earnestly from the heart.' The commitment of faith and hope must be worked out in earnest love – practical holiness.

We are all aware of the connection between faith, hope and love in Paul's writing. The same combination is found here. Is it surprising to find such close agreement between Paul and Peter? They were very different characters, but they knew the same Lord and shared the same beliefs. Their similar emphasis indicates that the relationship between faith, hope and love is basic to Christianity. Faith and hope come first. They are necessary before anyone is fully incorporated into the Church by baptism. But unless they result in love they are empty ideas, void of practical content. [1 Cor 13:13]

Faith is the initial response, as well as being a gift from God. Hope springs to life immediately the response in faith is begun. It is part and parcel of a new, God-ward direction, the 'turning round' for which the technical term is 'repentance'. But none of this, no purification, no baptism, dedication, conversion, or calling is real, or even useful, unless it issues in love – love towards our fellows that springs from our love of God.

An old proverb states, 'the proof of a pudding is in the eating'. The proof of purification, baptism, dedication, conversion, calling, or any other aspect of the Christian life is in love. [TO PONDER]

THURSDAY 31 OCTOBER
A SPIRITUAL HOUSE

READING 1 PETER 2:1–5
'Like newborn babes, long for the pure spiritual milk . . . like living stones be yourselves built into a spiritual house, to be a holy priesthood, to offer spiritual sacrifices acceptable to God through Jesus Christ' (vv. 2a,5b, RSV).

TOGETHERNESS IN THE GOSPEL would be a fitting title for Peter's letter. Over and again he stresses the need for Christians to work together, and his illustrations often spell out the fact that solitary Christianity is a contradiction in terms.

v. 2   The initial craving for spiritual milk may appear to be a solitary process – but milk can only come where someone is on hand to provide it. As the spiritual experience of the Christian grows, the metaphors of togetherness increase. One stone on its own is useless. To build a
v. 5   spiritual house it is necessary for the bricks, the living stones, to come together. Only then can a vital structure, a vibrant community, be built.

A priest is one who mediates. Priesthood implies bringing together. The Latin word for priest 'pontifex' means a bridge builder. That sums up the priestly function – to build a bridge between man and God. Every Christian is a priest. Every Christian has the spiritual responsibility to be a bridge between man and God. It is not something we
2:9   can leave to a select few. We are all in it together. There is no longer a separate caste of priests, as under the Old Dispensation. Peter teaches that the holy priesthood is a spiritual priesthood, involving the whole Christian community.

TO PONDER   *The spiritual sacrifice we offer to God involves sacrificing our own desires, our own ambitions, our own thoughts and feelings. It involves handing them over to God, for him to use on behalf of others. This spiritual sacrifice is made by men and women alike. All are priests.*

FRIDAY 1 NOVEMBER
THE CORNERSTONE

READING 1 PETER 2:6–10
'I am sending Christ to be the carefully chosen, precious Cornerstone of my church, and I will never disappoint those who trust in him' (v. 6, LB).
'The stone rejected by the builders has proved to be the keystone, a stone to stumble over, a rock to bring men down' (v. 8, JB).

PETER continues by citing one of the New Testament's favourite Old Testament quotes (v. 8). The ideas in this section need taking alongside those earlier in the chapter. The cornerstone is part of a living structure. The Church is not just bricks and mortar, preserved for posterity like a museum. It is a living, developing, moving community in which relationships are built, where every part affects the other.

v. 8
Ps 118:22
Mark 12:10
Matt 21:42
Acts 4:11

The Jerusalem Bible uses the term 'keystone', continuing the picture of the bridge. It emphasises the mediating, priestly role of Christ and his Church. It also highlights the fact that a keystone is useless unless it forms the top of an arch. Without supporting stones the keystone falls into the chasm beneath to be swept away. Even Christ, the keystone, is supported by the rest. We can do nothing without Christ. Christ can do nothing without us.

JB v. 8

We mustn't take such pictures too literally, but it seems legitimate to press this one a little further. Isn't proper recognition of the role of the humble, ordinary person, a stumbling block for much of our Christian ministry? We ignore at our peril the reality that every single member of the Church is vital. Some of us may be visible, with a profile way above the water line. Others of us may just be tiny sections of the foundation, who feel submerged by the waters swirling around us. But without us the bridge would fall.

Christ alone cannot make the Church. He needs the support of every one of his humble brothers and sisters if the house, the bridge, or any other structure we use to give a picture of the Church, is to stand.

TO PONDER

SATURDAY 2 NOVEMBER
SUBMISSIVE ALIENS

READING 1 PETER 2:11–17
'As aliens and strangers in the world . . . Submit yourselves for the Lord's sake to every authority instituted among men . . . For it is God's will that by doing good you should silence the ignorant talk of foolish men' (from vv. 11,13,15, NIV).

CHRISTIANS ARE PILGRIMS. We are followers of a way, a way which runs counter to the values of this world. We cannot simply go along with the selfishness, greed and violence of human society. We must stand apart from it. Some do this, like the veteran Methodist preacher Donald Soper, by maintaining a completely pacifist stance. Others do it, like the modern martyr Archbishop Romero, by condemning oppression and calling for freedom. Some do it, like Sheila Cassidy, the Christian doctor who was imprisoned in Chile, by even-handed treatment of government official and 'terrorist' alike.

At the same time, Peter urges us to submit to every human authority. It seems an impossible request. Yet it is exactly as 'aliens and strangers' – that is as people who do not recognise the ultimate authority of the powers of this world, that we must submit to them. If we do not, if we simply oppose every human authority for the sake of showing our differences from those around us, we bring the Christian gospel into disrepute.

It is a difficult balance to maintain, the balance between submission to authority, and condemnation of the misuse of authority. It can only be maintained by distancing ourselves from the greed for power, by acceptance of a subordinate role, and by retention of the freedom to act under the Spirit's guidance, in the words of Jesus, as the 'salt' or the 'leaven' in society.

Matt 5:13
Luke
13:21 AV

TO PONDER *Submission to the law must never be used as an excuse to let up on Christian pressure for change where the law is bad. It must never be used as an excuse for silence when a good law is badly administered.*

SUNDAY 3 NOVEMBER
SUBMISSIVE SLAVES

READING 1 PETER 2:18–25
'Slaves, submit yourselves to your masters with all respect, not only to those who are good and considerate, but also to those who are harsh' (v. 18, NIV).

PETER'S WRITING is crystal clear. He requires Christians to submit to harsh and unjust treatment (v. 18), to accept any and every authority as God-given (2:13), and to regard endurance of unjust suffering (v. 20) as commendable for its own sake. That seems to be going too far! It puts Christians in danger and risks making dictators think they do good by persecuting Christians!

We cannot ignore Peter's advice. We must take the rough with the smooth, and not reject out of hand a statement that makes things hard for us. But equally we have to take it in context. Peter wrote to people who could do nothing about their situation. There was no way they could rise up and change society. Such change could only come from their example. Few of us are in such a situation. With some exceptions, under most oppressive regimes today there are ways that voices can be heard, and support given. We can do our part to change society in a way which was not open to the early Christians. If we sometimes feel powerless, they were even more so.

We need to take Peter's advice in the context of Paul's writings. Paul teaches that we can do nothing to bring about our salvation, so even suffering will not assure us of a place in heaven. What it will do is to identify us with our Lord. It will remind us that nothing can separate us from the love of God. With such positive thought, we can indeed endorse Peter's statements. Harsh and unjust treatment will not make us bitter, but will be used to show a different example to our persecutors.

PRAYER SUBJECT: *For a submissive spirit.*

PRAYER: *Lord, we are so often keen to justify ourselves, to seek for our rights, and to make a fuss if we do not receive our due. Make us submissive, Lord, to your will but help us to fight on behalf of others, for their rights, and for them to receive their entitlement.*

MONDAY 4 NOVEMBER
SUBMISSIVE PARTNERS

READING 1 PETER 3:1–7
'You wives must accept the authority of your husbands' (v. 1a, WB).

Col 3:18,19;
Eph 5:22,23;
1 Tim 2:9–15;
Titus 2:4,5

TO OBEY or not to obey? Several New Testament passages deal with husband–wife relationships. All stress the need for obedience. They reflect the customs of the age when they were written. Then it was unthinkable that women could have official authority over men, though women have always wielded a very strong influence through their domestic role even in the most male-dominated societies. Wives and mothers have influence, especially wives and mothers of those who claim to rule.

Gen 21:10

v. 6

Sarah, whom Peter uses as an example of a submissive wife, influenced Abraham to rid himself of Hagar, against his better judgement!

Nowadays things have changed. In 1858 Catherine Booth's comment in her pamphlet *Female Ministry* was shocking: 'Why should woman be confined exclusively to the kitchen and the distaff, any more than man to the field and the workshop?' Such thought is commonplace today. It is in accordance with the Scripture's witness that all people are equally valued in God's sight. No distinctions can be made. A relationship in which husband, in many things, obeys the wife is just as valid as one where the wife, in many things, obeys the husband.

'In the same way you husbands must live understandingly with your wives' (v. 7).

Try substituting in both highlighted passages, wife for husband and husband for wife. Parents and children, servants and masters, employers and employees, councillors and constituents – try a similar substitution to get at the essence of what Peter is saying about human relationships. There must be **mutual** respect and obedience.

TUESDAY 5 NOVEMBER
FINALLY!

READING 1 PETER 3:8–16
'Finally, all of you, have unity of spirit, sympathy, love of the brethren, a tender heart and a humble mind' (v. 8, RSV).

PETER PREACHED to himself. We all do it. The more we preach humility, the more likely it is that we are prone to pride. The more we shout about the need for purity, the more likely it is that our own tendencies are far from pure.

In today's list of good qualities, can we see some of the things Peter was prone to lack? I think we possibly can. He was argumentative – so needed to call for unity of spirit. He was sometimes unaware of others' feelings so needed to call for sympathy. Did he sometimes find it hard to love the brethren? Was he stern and proud? Note how he set off fishing when his hopes were dashed, instead of waiting for Jesus' words to him to be realised. Mark 8:32 / Luke 22:60 / John 21:21 / John 21:3

But God does not judge us according to what tempts us most. He knows our personalities differ. He knows some of us are tempted more in one direction than another. None of us can pride ourselves at not having the particular failing which we know has destroyed another.

Peter dictates this passage, exhorting his brother Christians to take upon themselves all the good qualities he knew were hardest for him, expecting it to be the culmination of his letter. But, as with so many preachers, his 'finally' comes half-way through. Many more thoughts well up in his mind to encourage the persecuted Christians of Bythinia and the other areas around the Black Sea. We can forgive him his over-enthusiasm, his continual repetition, as he encourages others to take on the qualities he himself tended to lack, knowing that at heart he was fully committed to his Lord, Jesus Christ.

Let us be as forgiving of our friends' failings, close to home, as we are of Peter's failings at this distance of time and space. AN EXHORTATION

WEDNESDAY 6 NOVEMBER
GOD'S GRACE – I

READING 1 PETER 3:17–22
'He was put to death in the body but made alive by the Spirit . . . Noah . . . (was) saved through water, and this water symbolises baptism that now saves you also' (vv. 18b,20,21, NIV).

WoL 15 Oct

THE EXODUS experience was part of the religious consciousness of the Jews. We have seen how it affected Ezekiel and the exiles. It was the supreme example for them of God's saving grace, working to fulfil the purposes of God for his chosen people. They were saved by passing through the waters of the Red Sea.

But Peter's illustration goes further back than that. Peter uses Noah, who also had an experience of salvation through water – a salvation that meant the survival, not just of God's chosen people, the Jews, but of the whole human race. Peter's interest goes beyond the bounds of Judaism to the whole world. But the picture he uses is still a picture from his own cultural background, adapted to a new purpose.

In a similar way, Peter views baptism as a matter of salvation through the water. The total immersion symbolises going into, and being rescued from the waters which would have engulfed Noah, or Moses, or – in Christian terms – any one of us, had it not been for the saving grace of God. Baptism is an illustration of the way God works with us.

None of us can save ourselves, whether we are baptised, christened, dedicated, confirmed – even if we are ordained, commissioned, consecrated or even enthroned. None of this is effective in itself, but only through the grace of God which we cannot measure. That is the point to stress. We can set no limits on Christ's saving
v. 19 activity. None of us is beyond his care.

TO PONDER *Salvation comes by the grace of God alone.*

THURSDAY 7 NOVEMBER
CONVERSION

READING 1 PETER 4:1–6
'You have had enough in the past of the evil things the godless enjoy – sexual sin, lust, getting drunk, wild parties, drinking bouts, and the worship of idols, and other terrible sins' (v. 3, LB).

PETER'S READERS were mostly new Christians, people converted from a licentious life-style typical of periods of rapid social change. Old values were breaking down. New values were taking their place. Christianity came as a breath of fresh air to people who had had enough of idolatry, partying, frivolity and 'fun'. They knew that the pleasures of this world are shallow and passing. They were prepared to suffer for the sake of their new-found faith.

We face similar conditions today. But Christianity is hardly seen as fresh or new by many who are tired of their present empty existence. It has two thousand years of history behind it, and a 'conservative', established organisation. Its concern for its own, material survival seems as great as that of other human organisations. The Church finds it hard to practise the theory of self-sacrifice, suffering and trust outlined in Peter's epistle.

Recently I talked with a young Christian who had been brought up in the faith. He spoke of envy at the way his non-Christian friends enjoyed life. He seemed to be treading the Christian path more from fear of final judgement than from a deep, sincere love of Christ and his Church. Yet he longed for a real conversion experience. Can this come to someone who has not enjoyed the pleasures of this world and found them wanting? Praise God, it can – but only if we Christians are willingly prepared to accept the suffering Peter describes with joy in our hearts, deeper than the joy the 'world' knows. v. 1

Help us, Lord, to suffer willingly, unconcerned about our own survival, or even that of the Church. Let our chief concern be for the good news of Jesus Christ, and the salvation he offers to all. A PRAYER

FRIDAY 8 NOVEMBER
NEW AGE

READING 1 PETER 4:7–11
'The end of all things is near. Therefore be clear minded and self-controlled so that you can pray. Above all, love each other deeply, because love covers over a multitude of sins' (vv. 7,8, NIV).

THE NEW TESTAMENT ushers in a new age. It anticipates the end of all things. Theologians debate whether New Testament writers expected the end in their own life times. They debate what 'near' means. Is the New Testament wrong? Or should 'near' be set in the context of eternity, where a thousand years are but an evening? In other words, is it to do with time or with attitude? Such debate is interesting and possibly necessary. We can't have much faith in a Christianity based on a complete misunderstanding of the world's situation!

Yet for us the important matter is not so much what 'the end of all things is near' meant to Peter or other New Testament writers. It is not even so much what the 'end of all things' meant to Jesus himself. For us it is important to look at the context of such statements.

Mark 13

When the end seems to be near, there is a tendency to panic. A kind of apocalyptic hysteria may set in. Normal activity ceases. Some people may simply wait for the end, losing all sense of purpose. But that is not the Christian way. The New Testament asks us to act always as if the end is near – that is, to act normally. It asks us to retain our clarity of mind; to be self controlled; to continue loving each other in the way Christ commanded us to. And that means operating according to Christ's own example of sacrificial self-giving.

2 Thess 2:1,2 3:11

v. 7
John 13:34
v. 8

TO PONDER *A modern (and doubtful) philosophical movement calls itself the New Age but the idea is at the heart of Christianity. Christ ushers in a new age of practical love, care and involvement with our fellows which is always beyond the thinking of the present age, however secular or religious the present age might be.*

SATURDAY 9 NOVEMBER
SIMPLE DIFFERENCES

READING 1 PETER 4:12–19
'Take care that none of your number suffers as a murderer, or a thief, a rogue or a busy-body!' (v. 15, JBP).

BUSY-BODIES INDEED! What a cheek, to bracket murderers and busy-bodies together, separated only by thieves and rogues. Busy-bodies can be the salt of the earth. They are people who are into everything; always working, usually for others; never still. Without them the world would practically stop. So why does Peter condemn them as though they should be locked up and given a life sentence? The key is again found by looking at a further translation. *NEB* says 'nor for infringing the rights of others'. How sad that those who are busiest in the cause of others, so often do infringe the rights of others.

v. 15

A busy carer, looking after handicapped people, may be tempted to get more done by treating all alike. Routine can become master instead of servant.

A hard-pressed social worker may exercise powers to place people in institutions, where a more difficult, more compassionate approach would enable them to stay at home.

A teacher, driven to distraction trying to cope with the impossible, may take refuge in demanding a certain standard from all pupils, regardless of their special needs.

You can think of other examples from your own situation. Such things occur easily. They happen insidiously, and avoiding them requires miraculous grace and understanding.

Busy-bodies risk murdering the independence, the individuality, the simple differences between people. It's still odd that Peter lists them together with murderers, but can we begin to understand what he is getting at?

TO PONDER

SUNDAY 10 NOVEMBER
ANXIETY AND CARE

READING 1 PETER 5:1–7
'Be shepherds of God's flock that is under your care, serving as overseers – not because you must, but because you are willing . . . Cast all your anxiety on him because he cares for you' (vv. 2,7, NIV).

YOUNG AND OLD ALIKE suffer from anxiety. The world has never been a completely secure, comfortable place. Disruption, disaster and death have always been close. Today powerful media voices and pictures bring the selected anxieties of the whole world right into our living rooms, every day. So we may appear to live in times of greater unease than ever before. The calm, ordered world of the past seems to have vanished, replaced by uncertainty, disorder and change.

However, we need only look in parish registers or visit a local cemetery to see how insecure life itself used to be. As a race we may feel insecure; individually we have less need for immediate anxiety than earlier generations. But whether we should be anxious or not, most of us still are.

Peter doesn't offer complete freedom from worry and care. He does give a command, though, to cast our anxiety upon Jesus. Again the context is important. Peter has just been talking about looking after others. There is scarcely anything more worrying than taking responsibility for other people and looking after them. Indeed, we can hardly take responsibility for another, because we can never fully gauge how another person is going to react to our pastoral care for them. That is as true within the family as within the church fellowship, the social work situation, the classroom, or wherever.

Knowing that taking responsibility is bound to cause anxiety, Peter still encourages all Christians to be responsible for others, gladly and without compulsion (v. 2).

PRAYER SUBJECT: *For freedom from anxiety.*

PRAYER: *All your anxiety, all your care,*
Bring to the mercy seat, leave it there,
Never a burden he cannot bear,
Never a friend like Jesus.

(E. H. Joy, SASB 246)

MONDAY 11 NOVEMBER
SHARED SUFFERING

READING I PETER 5:8–11
'Your enemy the devil prowls around like a roaring lion . . . Resist him, standing firm in the faith, because you know that your brothers throughout the world are undergoing the same kind of sufferings' (vv. 8b,9, NIV).

REMEMBER, THERE'S ALWAYS somebody worse off than you are. How annoying those words can be. Very often we want to feel that we're badly done to, and that our problems really are greater than those of other people. Sometimes it is a comfort to think that we are coping with more than the next person has to endure. We get a kind of inverted pride in managing our adverse circumstances, sometimes even in managing them alone.

Yet how comforting it is also to know that we are not suffering alone. We have already spoken of the terrible isolation of the leper and when we suffer, isolation does indeed make our suffering much, much worse. Many people find strength by joining with other victims. Hence the mushrooming of societies for sufferers of all kinds, battered wives, abused children, victims of cancer, the limbless, the hard of hearing, the aged – the list is endless.

WoL 6 Sep
Mark 1:35ff.

Overcoming isolation was one of the main values of the letters written by early Christians. Men like Peter, Paul, the writer to the Hebrews, and others, were able to reassure those who suffered that they were not alone. It was a comfort to know God, in Jesus, was with them – but equally it was a comfort to know that others were holding firm to the faith, despite enormous hardship.

> *Join hands then, brothers of the faith,*
> *Whate'er your race may be;*
> *Who serves my Father as a son*
> *Is surely kin to me.*
>
> *(John Oxenham, SASB 826)*

A VERSE

TUESDAY 12 NOVEMBER
PETER (AND SILAS)—11

READING 1 PETER 5:12–14
'With the help of Silas, whom I regard as a faithful brother, I have written to you briefly, encouraging you and testifying that this is the true grace of God . . . Greet one another with a kiss of love' (vv. 12, 14a, NIV).

WE COME BACK full circle, to Peter's need for help and support. Silas was with him, using his skill, being a channel of communication for Peter, bringing him into contact with a wider audience than he had hitherto enjoyed – wider even than when Peter preached on the day of Pentecost.

Yet despite growing numbers in the various churches Peter could still command the congregations to greet each other with a kiss. The congregation was a family, with close personal ties between the members. A kiss was the natural way to greet other members of the family.

In time the early habit was lost. Congregations grew larger; membership became more diverse; close, family feelings became less intense and greeting each other with a kiss more problematic. Non-Christian wives or husbands would hardly appreciate other men and women kissing their partners. The greeting became misunderstood. Attempts were made to retain something of what Peter intended. Regulations about men only kissing men, or women only kissing women, were introduced, or the custom was followed of kissing a crucifix which would then be handed round the congregation.

Recently more emphasis has been placed on 'the peace', the occasion when the congregation greet each other in the Lord's name. There is, of course, a danger that too close-knit a congregation may appear unwelcoming to those outside. It can make non-members feel they are coming into contact with some kind of exclusive club. While recognising that danger, let us welcome every attempt to bring congregations closer together in the peace and love of Christ. Peter has done his part. It is up to us to do ours.

Peace to all of you who are in Christ

ZECHARIAH

After sixty years in exile, the Jewish community in Babylon was well established. Many of them had prospered. Although they felt keenly the loss of their homeland, they had taken Jeremiah's advice, had built houses, founded businesses, gained access to the Babylonian civil service and made themselves a valued part of Babylonian society.

When Cyrus, in about 537 BC, gave them the opportunity to return to their homeland, although many accepted, many others stayed. This time the most powerful members of the community seem to have stayed in place, so it was a relatively small, weak band who made the journey back to Judah. They had with them a number of influential figures, but not enough to really establish themselves as the long-term controlling influence on Judean society. After an initial burst of activity, when the foundation of the temple was laid, work ceased. Incomers, who had taken over much of the running of Judean affairs, put pressure on to ensure that building of the temple ceased. For seventeen years the returned exiles were unable to proceed further with their ambitious plans.

Then Haggai and Zechariah surfaced. Where they came from, no one knows. Where they went to when their mission was accomplished, we are equally unsure. But for four years they preached, prodded, threatened and cajoled the people of Judah. They stirred the conscience of the people and made them ashamed not to help in the rebuilding. They calmed the authorities. They used every means at their disposal to further the aim of providing Judah once again with a religious centre fit for the worship of God.

Zechariah's practical approach to the matter of spiritual inspiration is examined over the next couple of weeks before we come to our advent reading, and our final study of the early chapters of Acts.

WEDNESDAY 13 NOVEMBER
CHANGE, CHANGE, CHANGE

READING ZECHARIAH 1:1–6
'Do not be like your forefathers ... They would not listen or pay attention to me, declares the Lord. Where are your forefathers now?' (vv. 4,5a, NIV).

THE GOSPEL REQUIRES CHANGE. Each study in this volume has included a call for change under the direction of the Spirit. Ezekiel called on people to change their ways. The central pivot of his work, I suggested, was repentance. It was then argued 'Repentance is possible, for God offers us the possibility of a change of heart. "The leopard cannot change his spots," but the Christian is a continual witness to the possibility of a change of heart.' *(WoL 22 Oct)*

In our New Testament study, too, the message was one of preparation and change. Mark insisted, from the beginning, that we need a different attitude from the attitude of those who have gone before. His record of John the Baptist showed this clearly. The comment stated, 'The way of the Lord still needs preparation. Anyone who wishes to understand and take hold of the good news of Jesus still has to change their attitude. Our own selfish values have to be turned on their head if the gospel is to have meaning for us, and have meaning for those around us. If we cling to our old ways, the gospel cannot spread. The gospel requires us to be continually renewed, and provides the power for that renewal day by day.' *(WoL 1 Sep)*

Comment on Peter's letter claimed that today 'Christianity is hardly seen as fresh or new by many who are tired of their present empty existence.' *(WoL 7 Nov)* But equally we saw hope in Peter's own changed situation. 'Only the power of God's grace was able to change Peter from a weak, wilful character into a spiritual leader of the people.' *(WoL 25 Oct)*

Zechariah's message is the same. Avoid the mistakes of your forefathers. Revolutionary change is needed. A change from the selfish, short-term values of this world, towards the selfless, eternal values of the next.

THURSDAY 14 NOVEMBER
PEACEFUL OR POWERLESS?

READING ZECHARIAH 1:7–17
'They reported to the angel: "We have been all over the world and have found the whole world lies helpless and subdued"' (v. 11, GNB).
'They reported to the angel of the Lord, who was standing among the myrtle trees, "We have gone throughout the earth and found the whole world at rest and in peace"' (v. 11, NIV).

OLD TESTAMENT TRANSLATORS have a hard task. Ancient manuscripts are difficult to read. And when they can be read, the meaning may be obscure. The words translated 'myrtle trees' in *NIV* are not found in the *Good News Bible* version because the *GNB* translators admit that they don't know what they mean. With other words, some meaning is known, but the full significance may not be. Simple words may mean quite different things. 'Peace' is one example.

We long for peace. We pray for peace. We perhaps think of peace as one of the great goals of civilisation. None has yet attained it, but it is there in the distance, beckoning us on. If we don't find peace here on this earth, we trust it will be there, available to us, and enjoyed by us in the next.

But one man's peace may be another man's oppression. I remember a friend returning from South Africa a few short years ago and talking of the sense of peace he found there as compared to the feeling of unrest which he had always been aware of during many years in East Africa.

In today's verses, most translations stick to the terms 'at rest' and 'in peace'. But *GNB* sees it differently. It sees Zechariah talking, not of peace which comes from God, nor of peace arising from independence and lack of outside interference, but of the peace of subjection. It speaks of being 'helpless and subdued'. The World's peace is an enforced peace of unwilling conquest.

Which peace do I enjoy? The peace of willing obedience to a Heavenly Father, or the peace at any price of subjection to this world's powers?

TO ASK MYSELF

FRIDAY 15 NOVEMBER
THE MIGHTY FALLEN

READING ZECHARIAH 1:18–21
'The Lord showed me four craftsmen. I asked, "What are these coming to do?" He answered, "These are the horns that scattered Judah so that no-one could raise his head, but the craftsmen have come to terrify them and throw down these horns of the nations"' (vv. 20,21, NIV).

WoL 14 Nov

ZECHARIAH'S VISIONS inspire revolution. The world, we have seen, was at peace – or subdued, according to the point of view taken. Zechariah realised that that peace was unsettled. Cyrus had granted the small nations of his Persian Empire more freedom than they had known for decades under Babylonian rule. Now, ten years after Cyrus' death, the small nations were flexing their muscles trying for still greater independence.

Judah's chief symbol of national and religious identity was the Temple. The Babylonians had destroyed the Temple almost seventy years before Zechariah began to prophesy. Without a temple, the Jews felt bereft. Rebuilding it would be like rebuilding the nation itself. But such a task seemed a forlorn one.

Zechariah's vision inspired him to take on the seemingly forlorn task. Horns were symbols of military might, aggression and empire. Under normal circumstances craftsmen would be no match for the military might or 'horns' of the Persian empire. But with diplomacy, care and the right kind of inspired leadership, Zechariah knew that the craftsmen would conquer. The Temple would be rebuilt, and the nation would be re-created, not by military might, but by the power of the Spirit directing skilled, manual workers.

TO PONDER *New materials and new machinery, new conditions, require new skills, both in design and operation. These skills still need inspired channelling into creative projects if the powerful forces of destruction are to be overcome.*

SATURDAY 16 NOVEMBER
AN OPEN CITY

READING ZECHARIAH 2:1–5
'"Jerusalem will be a city without walls because of the great number of men and livestock in it. And I myself will be a wall of fire around it," declares the Lord, "and I will be its glory within"' (vv. 4b,5, NIV).

THE MODERN TRAGEDY of Jerusalem is such that Zechariah's visions seem like a pipe dream at the moment. Divided, embattled, threatened from without and within, there seems little hope of Jerusalem living at one with its neighbours in peace and harmony. Throughout its history Jerusalem has experienced strife. But Zechariah's vision was not a pipe dream. His vision became almost a reality. In four years the Temple was rebuilt. But the city did not enjoy much real peace, even then.

In recent months and years we have seen unbelievable changes occurring within some of the seemingly most powerful, immovable regimes on this earth. Who would have imagined the shifts in the balance of world power that we have seen? Who would have thought that the world could change, almost overnight? Where two implacable superpowers once faced each other in a 'balance of terror', we now see a shifting, exciting, potentially peaceful yet presently insecure mixture of smaller groups, each feeling their way to independence and making their own relationships with their neighbours.

Such changes are bound to bring trauma. But they also bring hope. Things are not beyond hope, even in Jerusalem. Perhaps one day it will be a 'city without walls', peaceful and prosperous. Let us pray that it will be so.

Meanwhile, the part we can play to hasten such a day, is to remember that all worldly power and influence is temporary. Military action may bring about temporary change. But the lasting 'wall of fire' is a spiritual one.

God alone is the source of infinite, eternal protection. TO PONDER

SUNDAY 17 NOVEMBER
SHOUT AND BE STILL

READING ZECHARIAH 2:6–13
'Shout and be glad, O Daughter of Zion. For I am coming, and I will live among you . . . Be still before the Lord, all mankind, because he has roused himself from his holy dwelling' (vv. 10,13, NIV).

SHOUTING, making noise, celebrating our gladness in the Lord, is one of the joys of worship. 'Songs of Praise', a selection of hymns, usually sung by members of a number of congregations, is one of the most popular religious programmes on British television. The most popular of these popular programmes are those which include rousing hymns sung by an enthusiastic crowd.

Celebrating the Lord with joy and singing can indeed be a source of inspiration. It was for Zechariah's people. He encouraged them to praise and to shout, for the Lord was indeed coming – what an awesome thought!

That thought brings us up short in our noisy celebration. It takes our breath away, causes us to stop and to consider the implication of the Lord coming into our lives. No wonder Zechariah calls on his readers, a few moments later to be still before the Lord. Stillness is uncomfortable. We feel guilty if we are not 'doing' something, yet faced with the awesome majesty of God, we cannot in fact do anything. All we can do is to stop, to surrender to him and allow him to do his work.

That is the great thing about becoming aware of God. Our own strivings becoming unimportant. Our centre of consciousness alters. We may still enjoy the noisy celebration. We will still praise the Lord, but at the root of it all will be the awesome understanding that God has broken in upon us, and brought a stillness and peace which the world cannot disturb.

PRAYER SUBJECT: *For a deep quietness of spirit.*

PRAYER: *Father, your presence turns our world upside down. Our values have to change. We have to think differently. In all this turmoil of spirit, come with your deep peace to quieten our hearts and prepare us to listen to your voice.*

MONDAY 18 NOVEMBER
SAVED

READING ZECHARIAH 3:1–5
'The Lord said to Satan, "The Lord rebuke you, Satan! The Lord, who has chosen Jerusalem, rebuke you! Is not this man a burning stick snatched from the fire?" . . . Then he said to Joshua, "See I have taken away your sin, and I will put rich garments on you"' (vv. 2,4b, NIV).

ZECHARIAH'S VISIONS continue with a picture of Joshua, or Jeshua, the high priest, standing before the Lord. He is being accused by the Satan, the 'prosecutor' in the heavenly court. Whether he is being accused for his own sin, or as a representative of the people is not specially important. But the idea in the writer's mind was probably of Jeshua, the priest, representing the people.

Satan's task was to accuse. He was the angel in the heavenly court whose job was to go over the earth and to make sure that all was well. If it was not well, then he had to report back and bring an accusation agaijnt those who were upsetting the well-being of the earth.

Job 1:6ff.

Such tasks are never pleasant initially. But how quickly we can begin to revel in them. The more success we have in bringing prosecutions, the greater our desire to take the process further. I'm sure Satan was like us in that. But that is not the Lord's way. He does not require the prosecutor to be concerned simply with bringing the criminal to book. Instead, he asks us to look on the criminal who has been brought before the divine court as one who is on the brink of salvation, a burning stick snatched from the fire.

What a different picture! Instead of punishing or demanding retribution, the heavenly judge clothes the accused with new garments, garments of peace, justice and joy, and sends him back to witness to the mercy and might of God.

Justice is empty without the hope of salvation.   TO PONDER

TUESDAY 19 NOVEMBER
AN IDEAL SOCIETY

READING ZECHARIAH 3:6–10
'"In that day each of you will invite his neighbour to sit under his vine and fig-tree", declares the Lord Almighty' (v. 10, NIV).

JOSHUA OR JESHUA, the reformed criminal, is sent back to take charge of the Lord's people. Whether it is as an individual, the priest amongst God's people, or as a representative of the whole people (Judah the nation which is to convey God's message to the rest of the world) is again unimportant.

The point to note is that Zechariah holds out hope of a society in which justice reigns. The beautiful symbol he uses for this ideal situation is one where 'each of you will invite his neighbour to sit under his vine and fig-tree'. That implies that each and every member of society has a stake in that society. Each one has something he can call his own, and somewhere to invite his neighbour.

It is a society in which there is social equality. Not a society where greed predominates. It is a simple society, not because it avoids the use of the beautiful, complicated resources which God has opened up to our investigation, but because it has reached a stage where the relationship between people is right. The leader, Joshua, and his associates, are symbolic of things to come. They are to be servants, not just leaders.

And we know, in a way that Zechariah did not, that the ultimate leader, the ultimate servant of the Lord is one who is willing to deny himself, put his very life on the line for others, and go all the way to the cross.

TO PONDER *Men are motivated by the desire for economic and political power, by greed and self interest. Zechariah's picture of leadership and equality is unfashionable. But without self-sacrifice, salvation cannot be achieved.*

WEDNESDAY 20 NOVEMBER
VISIONS AND VOICES

READING ZECHARIAH 4:1–5,10b–14
'"Do you not know what these are?" "No, my Lord," I replied . . . "These seven are the eyes of the Lord, which range throughout the earth" . . . "What are these two olive branches beside the two gold pipes that pour out golden oil?" . . . "These are the two who are anointed to serve the Lord of all the earth"' (vv. 5,10b,12,14, NIV).

EIGHT VISIONS were received by Zechariah.

1.	The angelic horsemen	1:7–17
2.	Four horns and four craftsmen	1:18–21
3.	A man with a line, measuring Jerusalem	ch. 2
4.	Joshua, the high priest, in rags	ch. 3
5.	Two olive trees and a candlestick with seven lights	ch. 4
6.	A flying scroll	5:1–4
7.	A woman in a measuring basket	5:5–11
8.	Four chariots, pulled by different-coloured horses	6:1–8

Each vision ended with a message. Uniquely, this fifth vision has a message included within it as well. The message of verses 6 to 10 is so important it will be dealt with separately tomorrow. Today we concentrate on the vision of the seven eyes, and the two anointed.

The seven lights (eyes) emphasise that the Lord sees and knows everything. Nothing is hid from his sight. We are reminded of Ezekiel's vision studied earlier.

Ezek 1:18
WoL 4 Oct

But this all-knowing, all-powerful Lord has servants whom he anoints for special tasks. In Zechariah's mind were surely Joshua the priest and Zerubbabel the prince. They are pictured as olive trees, also a significant symbol. Olives were the source of oil, used to feed the people, and also as oil for lamps. It was their task to be the channel for bringing light to their people. A task for both religious and secular leaders throughout the ages.

v. 10
Ezra 3:2
Hag 2:23

THURSDAY 21 NOVEMBER
SMALL THINGS

READING ZECHARIAH 4:6–10a
'Who despises the day of small things?' (v. 10a, NIV).

SIX TIMES *The Soldier's Armoury* dealt with this passage in its 35-year history. Six times verse six was highlighted. It is, indeed, a highlight. It reminds us that positive change occurs. '"Not by might nor by power, but by my Spirit," says the Lord'. However, towering as it does above other verses, it may become over-familiar. Its beautiful message, repeated, may lose its force.

The message, though, is reinforced in the last verse of the inserted passage. 'Who despises the day of small things?' In a day when the accent is on massive power, increasing wealth, economic dominance and the all-pervasive influence of the market, we must remind ourselves of the value of small things. Not only tiny microchips which control massive machinery, but other things whose importance may not be quite so easily grasped, like the following little play, used as part of an education programme by women in East Africa.

The scene is outside a village home. A woman is milking her cow. A transistor radio plays in the background, the catchy Coca-Cola company song *I'd like to teach the world to sing in perfect harmony*, with its enticing visions of how all the world's children love Coca-Cola. A salesman enters and tries to persuade the woman to sell her milk so she has the money to buy coke. She is strongly tempted to sell. A health worker then enters. It takes an enormous amount of persuasion to convince the woman that although her children love the coke, their bodies need the milk. In the end she resists the temptation to buy the coke and instead gives her children the milk to drink. The audience, of course, cheer loudly, and hopefully get the message.

TO PONDER *Such a drama is a small thing against the powerful media machinery of international companies. But it is life-saving. Let us not despise the day of small things.*

FRIDAY 22 NOVEMBER
BALANCE

READING ZECHARIAH 5:1–4
'I looked again – and there before me was a flying scroll! . . . And he said to me . . . "I will send it out, and it will enter the house of the thief and the house of him who swears falsely by my name. It will remain in his house and destroy it"' (vv. 1,3a,4b, NIV).

WE HAVE ALREADY DISCUSSED how the all-seeing power of God is symbolised in Zechariah's vision of lights on a candlestick. Here Zechariah extends that symbolism from God himself to God's law. The scroll which flies into every house belonging to a thief or a blasphemer represents the power of the law to reach into every corner of society.

4:2
WoL 20 Nov

We know, in the light of Jesus' statements, the shortcomings of the law. But Zechariah lived at the beginning of an age where the law of God was going to be of immense importance to the Jewish people. It was going to bind them together during centuries when they would be oppressed in their own land, governed by people who did not recognise their law. They would be denied the right to political freedom. Morally and religiously, though, keeping to their own, that is God's, law would enable them to retain an independent spirit.

Mark
3:4 7:9–13

And God's law is double-sided. On one side the law is against the thief – the person who disrupts society by robbing his neighbour. On the other side the law is against the blasphemer – the one who disrupts relationships between man and God. These two elements, the social and religious, go hand in hand. For an oppressed people neither is effective without the other, and neither can be separated completely from the other.

Good law requires a balance between duties to God and to man. No interpretation of the law which leads to oppression of people in the name of God will stand the light of God's judgement. Evil will ultimately lead to banishment.

TO PONDER

SATURDAY 23 NOVEMBER
A BASKET OF WICKEDNESS

READING ZECHARIAH 5:5–11
'I asked, "What is it?" He replied, "It is a measuring basket." And he added, "This is the iniquity of the people throughout the land"' (v. 6, NIV).

Matt
13:24–30

RIGHT AND WRONG are not always easy to distinguish. Instead of knowing exactly at every point which is the right action to take, we are forced to struggle with many options. Many courses of action are open to us, some obviously good, some obviously evil, the vast majority somewhere in between. The New Testament, which holds out hope of ultimate salvation, recognises this in a particular way. Wheat and tares grow together, hard to tell apart, until the harvest time.

Here in Zechariah's seventh vision, however, there is no recognition of such difficulty. Everything is very clear-cut. Against a particular cultural background, within a small-scale society like that of Judah, such thoughts may be applicable. Against a wider background, things are not so easy.

Most of us like to find something or someone to blame for our own shortcomings. The ancient Hebrews recognised the need to transfer blame, and used a powerful atonement ceremony. The priest laid his hands on a goat, which was then sent off into the wildnerness, symbolically carrying the sins of the people. Zechariah achieves this shift of blame by packaging up the wickedness of Israel, in the form of a woman, into a measuring basket and taking it off where evil belonged – to Babylon. For himself, and for his hearers it was a powerful picture, but hardly one which we can use today – except as a warning never to think that it is possible to put evil into a package and get rid of it. The problem of evil finds no easy answer. It is something we struggle with throughout our lives, combating it through the power of the Spirit of Jesus, the Spirit of one whose struggle against evil led finally to his own victorious death on the cross.

SUNDAY 24 NOVEMBER
IN THE NORTH, TOO

READING ZECHARIAH 6:1–8
'Then he called to me, "Look, those going towards the north country have given my Spirit rest in the land of the north"' (v. 8, NIV).

COMMUNICATIONS IN AND FROM Judah were difficult. To the east, there were some small tribes, then a great desert. To the south was Egypt, of relatively minor importance at this time. To the west a narrow coastal plain, and then the sea. The Judeans were certainly not seafarers. So it was to the north that Judah looked for communication with the rest of the world.

It was also from the north that the greatest threat to Judah came. There was no other way. Jeremiah talks of a boiling pot tilting away from the north (Jer 1:13). Anything coming from the north was trouble. Although Babylon lay east of Judah, the desert formed a barrier. No force of any size could come from the east. Babylon could only be reached by going round the fertile crescent, which meant starting towards the north. Equally, Judah could only be reached by an invading army from the north. The Babylonians and their successors, the Persians, always attacked from the north.

So to see the Spirit of the Lord going to reside in the north is quite remarkable. It is a complete contradiction of the previous vision of wickedness going packaged up to Babylon. If the Spirit of the Lord can be found in the north (that is in the land of Judah's religious as well as political enemies) then the Spirit of the Lord can be found anywhere. It is a point we do well to take notice of. It was a point the Pharisees found difficult to take when Jesus made it with regard to Samaritans. The Lord is with those whom we least expect him to be, and the Lord works through the most unlikely people.

PRAYER SUBJECT: *For the ability to cope with the unexpected.*

PRAYER: *We become aware of your presence, Lord, in the most unexpected places. Keep us continuously sensitive to your Spirit, whatever unexpected joys or sorrows come our way.*

MONDAY 25 NOVEMBER
WHO BUILDS?

READING ZECHARIAH 6:9–15
'This is what the Lord Almighty says: "Here is the man whose name is the Branch, and he will branch out from his place and build the temple of the Lord"' (v.12 NIV).

THOSE GIVEN CREDIT for building are hardly ever the people who actually do the work. An architect, a designer, or more often these days a financier, is credited with building.

Workmen who deal with a small portion of the building would be lost without the architect's design and oversight of the building as a whole. Great skill is required to ensure that the building works, fulfils the purpose for which it is intended, and stays up! The one who provides finance also has an overall part to play in the building; though to say he built it is a bit far-fetched.

Additionally there may be people involved neither in design, nor even in financing the work, who give the authority for it to go ahead. They, too, are part of the construction team. The Branch described in today's reading was one such. He was the one who would inspire the building, give authority for it to go ahead, and make sure it came to completion. Zechariah seems to have expected a kingly figure to guide the Temple through to its final form, using authority given to him by God.

We have no idea of his identity, but whoever he was, a historical figure, or a spiritual ideal fashioned by Zechariah the prophet, the work went ahead. Heldai, Tobijah and Jedaiah financed the project. It became their memorial. But it was Zechariah and the 'the Branch' who inspired the building.

A THOUGHT *Building is more than placing brick upon brick. It needs careful planning, thought and finance. But perhaps most important of all is the need for inspiration in order to force ideas into practical shape.*

TUESDAY 26 NOVEMBER
MOTIVE FOR FASTING

READING ZECHARIAH 7:1–7
'When you fasted and mourned in the fifth and seventh months for the past seventy years, was it really for me that you fasted?' (v. 5b, NIV).

IN TIMES OF CALAMITY in the Old Testament, there was a tendency to proclaim a fast. Even then, however, it was not a particularly common practice, and there seems to be no general Old Testament obligation to fast. Similarly, there are instances of individuals like Nehemiah fasting at times of great spiritual and emotional stress.

Jer 36:9;
Joel 1:14
1 Sam 7:6
etc.

Neh 1:4

Fasting was used as a sign of guilt. It highlighted the unworthiness of the people to stand before God. The people appear to have believed that it was more possible to approach God and ask him for particular blessings when in a state of physical as well as spiritual hunger. Fasting was used as a sign of mourning, and here in Zechariah the people were mourning the loss of their city, their temple and their homeland. With the return to Judah, the question of fasting became a real one. Habits form quickly, and once a penance like that of a regular fast is imposed as a religious observance, it becomes hard to break the habit without seeming to be irreligious. Jesus was condemned as a wine-drinker and a wastrel when he declined to fast in the way that the Pharisees did. Even though their fasting had become habitual rather than significant.

Isa 58:3,4

Mark 2:18

Here in Zechariah some 'modern' thinkers wanted to question the need for fasting now that the homeland was being restored. It was a difficult problem, for the restoration was not complete. The answer was to look more closely at the motive behind fasting. If fasting is undertaken, not as a matter of self-discipline, but as an exercise directed towards a greater understanding of God, then it has some value. But when oriented towards the self, or towards some object other than God, it is counterproductive.

When I deny myself something, is it in order to feel better in myself, or to bring me into closer contact with God?

TO ASK
MYSELF

WEDNESDAY 27 NOVEMBER
MOTIVE FOR MERCY

READING ZECHARIAH 7:8–14
'This is what the Lord Almighty says: "Administer true justice; show mercy and compassion to one another. Do not oppress the widow or the fatherless, the alien or the poor. In your hearts do not think evil of each other"' (vv. 9,10, NIV).

WoL 21 Nov

TODAY'S PASSAGE, TOO, towers above the rest of the text in its particular setting. Justice, mercy and compassion are such vital qualities, such overwhelming ideals, that they make our strivings after other, lesser goals, seem quite insignificant. Or do they?

It is impossible to guess what issues will be 'news' as you read this, more than a year since the words were written. But in the intervening year have we in the Church turned our back on petty squabbling over the ordination of women in order to provide an effective voice concerning the Gulf crisis?

Have we stopped fighting each other over the validity of infant or believer baptism, in order to concentrate our efforts on bringing hope to the hungry?

Have we forgone our vicious squabbling over the reality or otherwise of miraculous healing, in order to provide an effective healing ministry across the whole spectrum of endeavour? These and other questions must be answered – or rather acted upon – if our witness is to be effective.

Micah 6:8
Hosea 6:6
Amos 5:24
Jer 22:3
Ex 22:21,22

Again and again the Old Testament emphasises the qualities of justice, mercy and compassion, without which we cannot stand before God. Again and again the people get bogged down in trivial questions of ritual observance, keeping to the letter of the law, putting the spirit behind them. By not listening to the spirit, and concentrating on the application of the letter of the law instead, the land was 'left so desolate behind them that no-one could come or go'.

A PRAYER *Preserve us, Lord, from such deafness in these troubled days.*

THURSDAY 28 NOVEMBER
TRUTH – 1

READING ZECHARIAH 8:1–8
'Jerusalem will be called the City of Truth, and the mountain of the Lord Almighty will be called the Holy Mountain' (v. 3b, NIV).

A BEAUTIFUL PICTURE of peace, prosperity and truth is painted in this passage. Zechariah waxes lyrical about his vision of the future of Jerusalem. How saddened he would be to see that city today, torn apart by strife, wracked with rival perceptions of the truth so different from each other that it becomes impossible to assess the city's real condition; impossible even to guess what is fact and what is fiction.

Yet Jerusalem is still the city of truth. Jews, Muslims and Christians each venerate the city in their own way and associate it with the revelation of truth as they understand it. It was in Jerusalem that Christ's own perception of the truth brought about his condemnation and crucifixion. A city of truth, certainly, but how different from Zechariah's ideal!

Jesus talked in the upper room, in Jerusalem, about the 'Spirit of truth . . . who will guide you into all truth'. *John 16:13* Spreading out from Jerusalem, from the cross, and from Jesus' resurrection, the Spirit of truth has burned in the hearts of generations of Christians. We pray today for that Spirit to come, not just to Jerusalem, but here, where we are in the rough and tumble of our everyday lives.

> *Come, gracious Spirit, heavenly dove,*   A VERSE
> *With light and comfort from above,*
> *Be thou our guardian, thou our guide;*
> *O'er every thought and step preside.*
>
> *The light of truth to us display*
> *That we may know and choose thy way;*
> *Plant holy fear in every heart*
> *That we from God may ne'er depart.*
>   *(Simon Browne, SASB 190)*

FRIDAY 29 NOVEMBER
A CONNECTION?

READING ZECHARIAH 8:9–19
'The seed will grow well, the vine will yield its fruit, the ground will produce its crops, and the heavens will drop their dew . . . These are the things you are to do: Speak the truth to each other, and render true and sound judgment in your courts' (vv. 12,16, NIV).

WHY DOESN'T GOD do something? How often people ask such a question. Perhaps even more often they try to justify their unbelief by condemning God for doing nothing against the evil of this world. Men expect miracles to rescue them from the effects of their own failure, as well as from the forces of nature. But God rarely, if ever, intervenes in that way. His intervention is through the sacrifice of Jesus – quite a different matter.

Yet God does want to heal the sick – so usually he uses doctors. God does want to give abundant harvests – to do that he uses farmers. God does want to feed the hungry and clothe the naked – to do that he uses dedicated workers. It is in such ways that the grace of God is released to men.

We may argue that in spite of man's best efforts, still there is famine. But we only need to think for a single moment about the resources used for military purposes. Compare them with those used for famine relief, and we quickly see that the fault lies, not in God, but in man. We are always being told it is too simplistic to think in terms of comparing military expenditure (average 6 per cent of gross national product in countries around the world) with expenditure on relief (average less than half of one per cent). But the imbalance is so marked that we can hardly avoid making such comparisons.

TO PONDER *As individuals our contribution to truth, justice and mercy may seem paltry and insignificant, but unless individual Christians speak the truth, act justly, and show mercy, we can hardly expect God to intervene to save mankind from its folly.*

SATURDAY 30 NOVEMBER
TRUTH – II

READING ZECHARIAH 8:20–23
'This is what the Lord Almighty says: "In those days ten men from all languages and nations will take firm hold of one Jew by the hem of his robe and say, 'Let us go with you, because we have heard that God is with you'"' (v. 23, NIV).

THE JEWISH COMMUNITY was easily identified. Their God was a jealous God, who allowed worship of no other. He made stringent demands. They had to keep to dietary laws. They must circumcise their male children. They were obliged to sacrifice in a particular manner. They had to be careful whom they married, and not go outside well defined limits in their choice of a partner. We could hardly think of a group more exclusive and less likely to attract others.

Yet Zechariah prophecies that Jews will be envied, and their God sought after, not just by a few here and there but by ten people for every one of them. God has fulfilled this prophecy not ten times but thousands of times, in Jesus Christ.

What has attracted people in such numbers? And what has caused so many to turn away? Surely it is the truth. Truth is like a magnet which in certain conditions will prove a powerful attraction, and in others will repel. How easy it would be if we could simply say the sincere are attracted, and the insincere repelled by Zechariah's God, the God of the Jews who made himself known to us in Jesus Christ. But it is not so simple. The attraction is there, but so often our imperfect understanding of the truth causes sincere seekers to be repelled – and on occasion attracts the bogus and insincere.

Let us pray that the Church's sincere search for understanding will attract others to the truth of the gospel, and that even though we may not find all the answers, our search will bring others closer to our Lord and Saviour, Jesus Christ.

FOR PRAYER

SUNDAY 1 DECEMBER
SEEING IN THE DARK

READING 1 JOHN 1
'No longer will the sun be your light by day or the moon be your light by night; I, the Lord, will be your eternal light; The light of my glory will shine on you' (Isaiah 60:19, GNB).

OUR SPEECH is full of symbolism: we suffer a broken heart, give a cold shoulder, and turn over a new leaf. Our Christian faith and worship is also full of symbolism for we are unable to express our religious experiences adequately, or speak about the great truths we share, without turning to poetry. During Advent, at the start of the Church's calendar, we rely heavily on the symbolism of light. Even those who would not normally feel happy about lighting a candle in worship do so with a quiet heart at this time of the year. 'God is light and there is no darkness at all in him' (v. 5). In light, inaccessible, God may well be hidden from our eyes but we come to know him through Jesus who is spoken of as the light of the world. We associate light with warmth, protection, safety and guidance.

Darkness, on the other hand, with all its primitive associations, is equated with sin, its consequences, and the absence of God's presence in our lives.

The purpose of Advent is to encourage us, through readings from the Old and New Testaments, to prepare ourselves for the celebration of Jesus' first coming to earth; then to increase our longings and expectations for his return at the end of the world. In the meantime, God is our light and neither the sun nor the moon can shed more light on our path than the light of his presence shining around us, in us and through us.

PRAYER SUBJECT: *For spiritual enlightenment.*

PRAYER: *Heavenly Father, help me always to see your reality behind the religious symbols and language I use so easily. Through the leading of your Holy Spirit, guide me in this time of spiritual preparation so that I may understand better just what the mystery of Jesus' coming can mean for me and this world. Amen.*

MONDAY 2 DECEMBER
SPIRITUAL POWER

READING ACTS 1:1–8
'It is not for you to know the times or dates the Father has set by his own authority. But you will receive power when the Holy Spirit comes on you; and you will be my witnesses in Jerusalem, and in all Judea and Samaria, and to the ends of the earth' (vv. 7,8, NIV).

ACTS OF THE APOSTLES, or as some say, *Acts of the Holy Spirit* is Luke's second volume of a single work. The first we call Luke's gospel. The second continues the same story, but the emphasis shifts from Palestine to the whole world. The power manifest in the first volume, mainly in the area where Jesus was physically present, is now seen to extend beyond the boundaries of Jerusalem, beyond Judah, beyond Samaria, and out to the ends of the earth.

That power is spiritual. Spiritual power has nothing to do with force, with physical violence, with control of one person by another. Spiritual power is the power of reconciliation. In Christ we become one.

It is impossible to outline a definite, single method of discerning the presence of spiritual power in a community. But one clear sign of the presence of spiritual power is that the community will contain different kinds of people. In worldly society like attracts like, but spiritual power is magnetic; it attracts opposites to each other. In a community vibrant with spiritual power one will find the Pharisee and the tax-collector together; the Jew and the Samaritan; the stockbroker and the bikie; handicapped and able-bodied; employed and unemployed; young and old; married and single – and so we could go on. A discrete, homogeneous group is almost by definition bereft of spiritual power. They may wield wide influence, they may be numerically, economically or even religiously strong, but for spiritual power there must be a reconciliation between people beyond the attraction of like for like.

Luke 18??

The magnetism of the gospel attracts opposites into community. TO PONDER

TUESDAY 3 DECEMBER
THE ASCENSION

READING ACTS 1:5–12
'After he said this, he was taken up before their very eyes, and a cloud hid him from their sight' (v. 9, NIV).

LUKE MARKS THE BOUNDARY between volumes one and two of his work by his account of the ascension. Volume two, Jesus' heavenly ministry, is a natural sequel to volume one describing Jesus' ministry on earth. As William Barclay puts it 'The ascension stands for the final liberation of Jesus from all limitations of space and time.' It is a wonderful story, but only half a story. The full story is that Jesus, liberated from limitations of space and time returns to us **in** space and time through the ministry of the Holy Spirit. One day, then, we shall also be liberated as he was.

Our liberation is a spiritual liberation, already present in part as we enjoy the spiritual power Christ puts at our disposal. Spiritual liberation affects our life here on earth. It means we live in community with others, not under the domination of others, for our only Lord is the risen Christ. We accept the authority of the state, but its authority is never final. We accept we are unable to do many things we might want to do, but such limitations do not burden us with guilt for we know that in him all things are possible.

We may not be able to do what we want; perhaps not recover physical or mental health as we might wish, but none of these things are paramount. Christ's healing, Christ's call to special ministry, and his intervention in the lives of his disciples, have always been selective. He liberates us, not so much from the things themselves as from their domination. They may still be present, but in the liberated life there is always something more, the very presence of the Holy Spirit guiding, directing, and strengthening wherever we are.

TO PONDER *No longer is Jesus limited by time and space. He is here with us **now**.*

WEDNESDAY 4 DECEMBER
PRAYER PLUS

READING ACTS 1:13–26
'"Judas, who served as guide for those who arrested Jesus – he was one of our number and shared in this ministry" . . . Then they prayed, "Lord, you know everyone's heart. Show us which of these two you have chosen to take over this apostolic ministry"' (vv. 16b,17,24,25a, NIV).

THE TWELVE were bereft. Jesus had risen. They had rejoiced in his presence for a few short weeks following the resurrection. But now he was gone from them again. They knew his Spirit was with them, but however strongly a spiritual presence is felt, it never quite seems to replace a person's physical presence. If that were not so we would hardly mourn the departed, nor grieve when our loved ones were far from us.

But there was another reason for the post-ascension feeling of depression. With Jesus present in the flesh they had hardly missed one of their number, Judas. As soon as Jesus went they also missed Judas. The Twelve were reduced to eleven. Eleven was not a number they could identify with. The Twelve could picture themselves as a new Israel. As eleven they felt a poor imitation of the real thing. For their own peace of mind, and the furtherance of the gospel, they had to make the number up to twelve once again.

They prayed about it. They asked for guidance. They also acted. Two obvious candidates presented themselves, Barsabbas Justus and Matthias. There was little to choose between them. They were both, most importantly, witnesses to the resurrection. They were both reliable, worthy individuals who would ably fill the position vacated by Judas. How to choose? In accordance with their custom they drew lots. Prayer had guided them so far. It had taken them in the right direction. But sometimes, beyond prayer, an arbitrary decision must be taken.

Let us make decisions carefully, prayerfully, and then bravely. TO PONDER

THURSDAY 5 DECEMBER
INDIVIDUALS TOGETHER

READING ACTS 2:1–4
'When the day of Pentecost came, they were all together in one place
... They saw what seemed to be tongues of fire that separated and
came to rest on each of them' (vv. 1,3, NIV).

ALL AND EACH are the key words in this, one of the best-known passages in the whole of Scripture. It always surprises me how short the description of this Pentecost experience is. Four brief verses; nothing more; just a tiny filler at the bottom of a newspaper column, yet its effect has been world-shattering.

The disciples were together. They shared a common experience. They were united in aim and purpose. Such unity is necessary for the manifestation of the Spirit in full power. But the Spirit came to each individually. None were missed when the tongues of fire came to rest on them. The coming of the Spirit is personal, yet the personal cannot be separated from the communal.

When the Spirit was given there was no distinction between them in power. Yet we shall see in tomorrow's reading that Peter still took the lead. He had the public position but no monopoly of power. In material terms he was the strong, public leader. Spiritually, the least of the disciples was his equal. Such a statement seems commonplace. But it has to be stated over and over and over again, for our natural tendency is to venerate the public figure, to bow to the powerful individual, to honour him (or her) and give him a feeling of worth in accordance with the public image.

We naturally value our own more than others. It is partly instinct, partly security, partly familiarity. But in the eyes of God all are of equal worth regardless of our gifts and achievements. That is the measure of God's love for us. He values us each so highly that he offers us his Spirit; all and each; each and all in community, yet completely individually.

A PRAYER *Lord, give me your Spirit and make me free to serve you.*

FRIDAY 6 DECEMBER
MEANING

READING ACTS 2:5–16
'Amazed and perplexed, they asked one another, "What does this mean?"' (v. 12, NIV).

UNDERSTANDING REQUIRES MORE than grammar and vocabulary. It has to do with meaning. I am English. I know when someone is talking English, and generally claim to understand English. But often I find it hard to understand the meaning of what is said or written. Sometimes you, the reader, find it hard to understand what is written in *Words of Life* even if you know the meaning of each word used. Sometimes an unfamiliar word clouds the meaning of a whole sentence or paragraph; or a succession of lengthy syllables may be the cause of comprehension difficulties. (A lot of long words can make it hard to read).

Each who heard the first disciples at Pentecost 'heard them speaking in his own language'. Perhaps that meant that amongst the disciples were people who spoke each of the languages listed. Perhaps it meant that by a miracle the disciples were able to talk in foreign languages. Or perhaps it meant that the disciples and those who heard were using a language like the language associated with the gift of 'tongues'. Not enough detail is given for us to be sure.

v. 6

vv. 9–11

But however they understood what was said, those who listened were still perplexed. They still didn't know the real meaning of what they were hearing. They could not understand its significance. Not, that is, until Peter stood up and spoke to them. He explained that the outpouring of the Spirit they were witnessing was a fulfilment of the prophecies of Joel.

v. 14

Joel 2:28–32

Today people need an explanation of the gospel as convincing in their terms as Peter's was to his hearers if they are to understand it. Let us pray for wisdom and courage to expound the gospel clearly, simply and with conviction, to our modern age.

TO PONDER

SATURDAY 7 DECEMBER
A GIFT FOR ALL

READING ACTS 2:17–21
'In the last days, God says, I will pour out my Spirit on all people. Your sons and daughters will prophesy, your young men will see visions, your old men will dream dreams' (v. 17, NIV).

Jdg 6:34
Jdg 13:25
1 Sam 10:10
Ezek 2:2 etc.

THE ACTIVITY OF THE SPIRIT in the Old Testament was limited. Specially chosen, particular people – prophets, kings, sometimes even priests, were visited with a certain gift and moved by the Spirit. For instance Gideon, Samson, Saul, Ezekiel and others. But there was no widespread manifestation.

Joel 2:28–32

When Peter spoke on the day of Pentecost and related the unique Pentecost experience to the general outpouring of the Spirit prophesied by Joel, Peter himself assumed the Spirit would only be given to Jews. He did not learn properly that the gift would be given to others until after his contact with Cornelius.

Acts 10:47

But, as we often find with prophecies, Peter spoke truer than he knew. God was intervening and acting in a new way beyond even Peter's understanding.

Peter had, probably quite unconsciously, put a limit on the very outpouring of the Spirit that he was proclaiming. He could not yet take it on board fully. We ourselves, after almost 2,000 years still find there are certain parts of Joel's unique vision, proclaimed by Peter, that we do not take on board fully. How many Christian communities, including Salvationist ones, accept fully and completely that the Spirit is poured out on men and women alike? How many of us take seriously the statement that all who call on the name of the Lord will be saved?

TO PONDER *Do I take seriously the notion that the Holy Spirit is available for all? Do I proclaim this by my words, and by my actions?*

SUNDAY 8 DECEMBER
NO LIGHT – NO HOPE

READING JOHN 1:1–14
'The true light that gives light to every man was coming into the world' (v. 9, NIV).

DARKNESS CAN BE very frightening and our circumstances are usually perceived as being more tragic, more hopeless and much worse when it is dark. Generally speaking, when there is no light there is no hope. In the beginning when darkness covered the earth, God took action and created light.

The psalmist came to the conclusion that even in the dark there was no escape from his God: 'Even the darkness will not be dark to you; the night will shine like the day' (Ps 139:12). When Jesus was crucified a darkness covered the land but in that blackness God was at work bringing an even greater light within our reach and experience: God was redeeming the world to himself. In all our 'darkness', when it would appear that evil is gaining the upper hand, God is there creating light. He uses these moments for his glory and our great salvation. Is it not so, that after coming through a difficult chapter in our lives it is only then that we realise just how close God was to us, giving light to our path and saving us?

We must never forget that God is coming towards us however dark the moment might be.

Today's Bible reading declares that Jesus gives light to every one that comes into the world, and his light is so bright and strong that all the darkness imaginable can never put it out. There may be plenty of darkness in our lives, but there is even more divine, inner light to chase it away. Those of us who walk in the light, however dark it might become around us, always have hope. Praise be to God!

PRAYER SUBJECT: *That spiritual enlightenment may come to particular people.*

PRAYER: *Father of light, in this moment I pray by name for people who feel that their lives are overtaken by darkness. In particular I pray for . . . . and ask that the light of Christ will enlighten them.*

MONDAY 9 DECEMBER
REMEMBER HIS EXALTATION!

READING ACTS 2:22–36
'God had already decided that Jesus would be handed over to you; and you killed him by letting sinful men crucify him. But God raised him from death . . . God has raised this very Jesus from death, and we are all witnesses to this fact. He has been raised to the right-hand side of God, his Father' (vv. 23,24a,32,33a, GNB).

THE HOLY SPIRIT'S PRESENCE was central to Peter's message. But when we stress too strongly that the Spirit is available, here and now, for everyone; when we stress too strongly the indwelling power of the Holy Spirit; when we over-emphasise the nearness (immanence) of God, then we run the risk of forgetting that God is also supreme. And if Jesus is to reflect the nature of God completely; if Jesus is to bring us into contact with God, then, as well as recognising him to be near, we must also recognise him as supreme.

v. 33a, 5:31
7:55 9:3,5

So Peter and others in the early Church were careful to point out how Jesus was exalted to the right hand of God. He is near, he is also far. He is with us, he is also with God. He is immanent, he is also transcendent, to put it in theological language.

The exaltation of Christ and the outpouring of the Holy Spirit form a single whole. The gift of the Spirit takes for granted the fact that Jesus is present, interceding with the Father on our behalf. It takes for granted the fact that our salvation is assured.

v. 36b
v. 36b RSV

So we can affirm, along with Peter, the closing words of his speech. 'Know for sure that this Jesus, whom you crucified, is the one that God has made Lord and Messiah!' or, in another version, 'God has made him both Lord and Christ, this Jesus whom you crucified.'

TO PONDER. *Whenever I feel the Spirit's power within me, I must also recognise the Lordship of Christ over me.*

TUESDAY 10 DECEMBER
ACTION

READING ACTS 2:37–41
'When the people heard this, they were cut to the heart and said to Peter and the other apostles, "Brothers, what shall we do?"' (v. 37, NIV).

INITIAL REACTION to the Christian message may be a reaction of despair. Sometimes it is possible for a preacher to load his congregation with a sense of guilt, a real feeling of responsibility for the death of Christ himself, so that if he is not careful his hearers can be reduced to a kind of frozen state, solidified by guilt and unable to act.

'Brothers, what shall we do?' seems to be just such a cry of despair. It seems to expect the answer 'Nothing, there is nothing that you can do'. In one sense, of course, that is true. We cannot save ourselves. God has done it all for us.

v. 37

But in another, just as real sense, we must act. We must repent, turn in a different direction – that is towards Jesus – and start to 'Save yourselves from this corrupt generation'. Part of the action of 'saving ourselves' is to repent. Another part is witnessing to the change. Baptism is such a witness, associating ourselves with the body of Christ, which is his Church. But whether it be by baptism, by confirmation of an earlier, infant baptism, or perhaps by enrolment as a soldier within that part of the Church which is The Salvation Army, the important thing is that we witness to the change by becoming part of a fellowship of believers.

v. 40

v. 38

In normal conditions, Christ has little use for silent, solitary believers. They are abnormal. Sometimes, tragically, the world forces Christians to be silent and solitary. Christianity then has to become a matter of sheer, dogged, personal faith, in isolation from other believers. But such situations are conditions against which every Christian will strive, and rejoice when the freedom to witness is gained once more.

WEDNESDAY 11 DECEMBER
A PERFECT PATTERN

READING ACTS 2:42–47
'All the believers were together and had everything in common. Selling their possessions and goods, they gave to anyone as he had need' (vv. 44, 45, NIV).

Matt 16:28
Mark 13:30
14:61,62
1 Thess 4:15–17
Rev 1:1 etc.

THE FIRST CHRISTIANS believed the end of the world was near. They were convinced Jesus would return in their lifetime. It was therefore relatively easy for them to pool resources, meet together for prayer and worship, breaking of bread and fellowship, and wait for the end to come.

Even in that situation disputes soon broke out. Within months, perhaps weeks, complaints arose that Grecian widows were being overlooked in the general distribution, while those with Hebrew backgrounds were getting more. So specialised administrators had to be chosen to oversee the distribution. A bureaucracy was being put in place!

Acts 6:3

It is easy to mock efforts at communal living and equal distribution. It is just as easy to idolise them. Instead, look to them as a pattern for the organisation of society, setting out the goal, if not the detailed means to achieve it. The goal is surely equality – a dirty word in some quarters these days – and the means to achieve it is through productive work and superb administration, backed up by the fellowship of prayer and worship. Each has a duty to contribute. And each has a right to receive. How we measure the balance between contributing and receiving for individuals, and for groups, will always be a matter of contentious debate. But the governing principle in the early Church was individual and group need, not individual and group greed. The governing principle is equality before God for the weak and the powerful, the individual and the group. With such principles governing a community many miraculous signs and wonders will indeed be done.

v. 43

TO PONDER *The morality of the market is no morality at all.*

THURSDAY 12 DECEMBER
RICHES

READING ACTS 3:1–10
'He asked them for money. Peter looked straight at him, as did John . . . Then Peter said, "Silver or gold I do not have, but what I have I give you. In the name of Jesus Christ of Nazareth, walk"' (vv. 3b,4a,6, NIV).

ONE DAY, it is said, a medieval Pope was with the scholar Thomas Aquinas, watching the revenues of Europe pouring into the Vatican. 'The time has gone,' said the Pope, 'when the Church had to say, "Silver or gold I do not have"' Thomas replied, 'The time has also gone when she could say to the paralytic, "But what I have I give you, arise and walk."'

Perhaps those who live in an affluent society should ask what links, if any, there are between these two facts. Is it true that material comfort often accompanies spiritual poverty?

Now material poverty itself does not create spiritual vitality. If we are sentimental about the delights of poverty, we have probably never experienced it. Poverty creates an obsession with making ends meet. Links between material poverty and spiritual wealth are not necessarily links of cause and effect. We should not develop a guilt complex about attaining a reasonable standard of living.

However, we must remain aware that material affluence *can* bring poverty. We may give of our resources, instead of giving ourselves. Put in stark terms as in the story of the beggar at the Temple gate, we can easily see that the gift of walking is better than successful begging. But our gift will usually be less dramatic. Most of us will be judged by the sincerity of a handshake, by our patience with difficult people, by devotion of time to caring, and a host of further, undramatic ways of giving ourselves to others.

TO PONDER

The cost of charity can not be assessed in monetary terms. Its true measure is the degree to which we give ourselves to others.

FRIDAY 13 DECEMBER
NOT ME, BUT HIM

READING ACTS 3:11–16
'It is Jesus' name and the faith that comes through him that has given this complete healing to him, as you can all see' (v. 16, NIV).

THE SPIRIT WITNESSES to Jesus. Although we talk, as we have in this volume, of the Spirit's inspiration, it is always to Jesus that the Spirit points. This, of course, is at the root of all spiritual discernment. Any spiritual movement or force which points in any direction but to Christ is to be avoided as counterfeit.

Human beings tend to glorify people through whom healing comes, whether it be healing of body, mind or spirit. Of course we thank the doctor for his efforts when he makes us well. Of course we appreciate what the psychiatrist achieves. And naturally we are grateful for wise counselling from friends, neighbours and professionals of all kinds. But if we then go on to believe that they have been the root cause of the healing, we go sadly astray.

The crowd came running to Peter and John, and stared at them as though they themselves had achieved the healing. Peter and John immediately turned their attention away from themselves and towards Christ. They claimed to have no power of their own. Their only power was the power of Christ working through them.

We may be grateful to Peter and John that they used this power – and that is all. The messenger can never replace the one who sends him. But how easy it is to be swayed by the adulation of the crowd into thinking that our use of the powers of Christ reflects some special credit on us. How easy it is to venerate preachers, sensational healers, influential pastors and others, when our attention should be turned to Christ himself.

TO PONDER *We can never remind ourselves too often that Jesus' name alone brings healing.*

SATURDAY 14 DECEMBER
PATTERN FOR PREACHING

READING ACTS 3:17–26
'God fulfilled what he had foretold through all the prophets, saying that his Christ would suffer. Repent, then, and turn to God, so that your sins may be wiped out, that times of refreshing may come from the Lord, and that he may send the Christ . . . even Jesus' (vv. 18–20, NIV).

PREACHING in the early Church followed a regular pattern. It was called the 'kerygma' or proclamation. Of course, each sermon varied. Some contained more material than others, but the initial proclamation made by Peter, Paul and others to these early gatherings of inquisitive, potential believers, follows a similar pattern, which is basic to the Christian message.

1. Old Testament prophecy has been fulfilled.
2. Jesus is the fulfilment of prophecy.
   a. Jesus lived, one of David's descendants.
   b. He ministered, performing mighty works.
   c. He died, on the cross.
   d. He rose again.
   e. He is now exalted, at God's right hand.
3. Jesus will come again.
4. So repent and be baptised.
5. And receive the Holy Spirit.

This pattern can be followed through in many New Testament passages, a few of which are listed here:

with just point three absent in Acts 2	2:14–39
with just point five absent in Acts 3	3:12–21
in different order, with just point three absent in Acts 4	4:8–12
in short form, missing point one and point three in Acts 5	5:30–32
spoken by Paul, missing points three and five in Acts 13	13:17–39
written by Paul, in shortened form, in 1 Corinthians	1 Cor 15:3–5

Look for other examples of this pattern of early preaching as you read the New Testament. It is the basis of our faith, looking back to the historical fact of Jesus' life and death; enjoying now the delight of his resurrection; looking forward to the hope of his coming again.

AN EXERCISE

SUNDAY 15 DECEMBER
. . . AND ON EARTH, PEACE

READING ISAIAH 9:2–7
'For he himself is our peace' (Ephesians 2:14, NIV).

EVEN THOUGH WE HAVE international peace-keeping forces, peace movements, peace studies and an international peace prize, we have yet to experience true peace on earth. And that is not God's fault for he is a God of peace and has done everything possible to give us this, his special gift. He wants peace for us his children much more than we apparently do. We may long for peace as an ideal, but then 'most ideals are alien to human nature'. More often than not we can be found standing in the way of our own ideals, especially in matters of peace, when the price is too high.

Peace is a basic attitude of life, a life-style, not a few loose principles for difficult situations or awkward relationships. The pursuit of peace may involve us in not only facing up to conflict, but even creating conflict in order to achieve the true goal.

Why has peace so long evaded us? Perhaps we have been so obsessed with achieving peace that we have shown no interest in the Prince of Peace – the source of all true peace. There can be no real peace except through knowing Jesus – it only comes through relationship with him.

So long as we keep things in the wrong order we shall never achieve peace. We first have to know him before we receive his gift. Advent is the announcement of peace for us all, in every situation, through coming to know him who is our peace.

PRAYER SUBJECT: *For peace.*

PRAYER: *Great Father of Peace, who sent your Son into the world to become our peace, forgive us when we have got in the way of your purpose for the world. Forgive us when we have avoided conflict for cowardly reasons, imagining that by so doing we were living peacefully. Grant us your peace which the world cannot give or know, in the name of the Prince of Peace, Jesus our Saviour. Amen.*

MONDAY 16 DECEMBER
SLOWLY, SLOWLY

READING ACTS 4:1-4
'They were greatly disturbed because the apostles were teaching the people and proclaiming in Jesus the resurrection of the dead . . . They put them in jail until the next day' (vv. 2,3b, NIV).

IDEAS ARE POWERFUL. They take root in the minds of people and alter their courses of action. While they remain simply ideas, they may be tolerated. Once they begin to be acted upon, opposition grows.

The idea that slavery was wrong was applauded – until Wilberforce and others began to insist that action should be taken. Then how the slave owners and others who saw their livelihood threatened, opposed!

The idea of world government is applauded – until attempts are made to put it into practice. Resolution after resolution is simply ignored with impunity.

Even the idea of European unity is fine as an idea, but how the nations oppose when action threatens their vested interests!

Opposition to the apostles started slowly, just one night in jail and a warning not to carry on with their outrageous practice of preaching and acting upon the new idea that Jesus was the Messiah. Gradually, as Christian activity increased and threatened to upset the vested interests of Temple authorities, opposition increased. Acts perhaps gives the impression that it happened in an instant. But there were months, perhaps on occasion even years, between the various events described. The Church itself, after initial bursts of growth, grew slowly. For many years it remained an underground movement, opposed at every turn. It made the establishment feel uncomfortable. It challenged authority, though it sought no overthrow of any legally constituted regime.

TO PONDER

Today, we do not seek opposition, any more than the early Church sought it. We do not threaten legally constituted regimes. But when the Church puts apostolic ideas into practice, opposition is bound to occur.

TUESDAY 17 DECEMBER
CHRIST ALONE

READING ACTS 4:5–12
'Salvation is found in no-one else, for there is no other name under heaven given to men by which we must be saved' (v. 12, NIV).

IN A WORLD where each of us is becoming increasingly affected by the presence of great religions other than Christianity, the claim made by Peter before the Sanhedrin can sound harshly dogmatic. How can we assert that Christ is unique?

Asserting the uniqueness of Christ does not deny the fact that God has revealed truth outside the Christian faith. The deep insights of other religions, and the real holiness of some of their devotees are indications that everywhere and at all times God has revealed truth to those who would receive it. John's gospel identifies Jesus with the eternal Word, and makes the claim that he enlightens every man. In what may appear one of the harshest of Jesus' parables we learn that when those who do not know him act lovingly towards the needy they are in fact encountering Christ.

John 1:9
Matt 25:31–46

We cannot confine God within the narrow, exclusive boundaries of the Christian Church, any more than the Jews could confine him within the bounds of an exclusive Pharisaism.

Yet we do claim that Christ is unique. His uniqueness is not expressed by excluding all other insights and goodness, but by knowing that Christ sums up and expresses to perfection, the truest and best.

A VERSE

> *There's no other name but this name,*
> *And no other name will do.*
> *There's no other name but Jesus*
> *For folk like me and you.*
> *For no other name brings pardon*
> *And sets everybody free.*
> *There's no other name but Jesus*
> *For you and me.*
>
> *(John Gowans, SASB 71)*

WEDNESDAY 18 DECEMBER
FEAR

READING ACTS 4:13–22
'"What are we going to do with these men?" they asked. "Everybody living in Jerusalem knows they have done an outstanding miracle, and we cannot deny it. But to stop this thing from spreading any further among the people, we must warn these men to speak no longer to anyone in this name"' (vv. 16,17, NIV).

THE AUTHORITIES, representatives of official religion, were afraid. Fear motivated their reaction to Peter and John. What would happen to the established order if Peter's and John's ideas took hold? We have already seen that ideas expressed in action threaten vested interests of all kinds. Fear affects the strong as much as, possibly more than, the weak.

We might expect wealth and power to bring a sense of security. But no, the opposite seems true. The more we have, the more we fear losing it. We go to great lengths to preserve power, and to protect what we have.

If we have nothing, we have nothing to lose. In one way then, the advantage is always with those who have nothing. It is they who are prepared to risk their very lives in causes they know (or think they know) to be right. It is they who will risk living according to the precepts of the gospel, for they have no property, power or influence to lose.

So authority fears new movements, for it is always possible the balance of power will move, and that the powerful will be dispossessed. Such fears lead to censorship, oppression and curtailment of the rights of others.

The Sanhedrin could not dispute that a lame man had been restored. But instead of rejoicing, they became more afraid. Nothing in the law condemned Peter and John, so they were reduced to ordering them to be silent.

TO PONDER
Whenever silence is ordered, we may suspect vested interests are involved which need to be examined and exposed.

THURSDAY 19 DECEMBER
POWER

READING ACTS 4:23–31
'Herod and Pontius Pilate . . . did what your power and will had decided beforehand should happen. Now, Lord, consider their threats and enable your servants to speak your word with great boldness' (vv. 27a,28,29, NIV).

GOD CREATED the heavens and the earth. What greater manifestation of power could there be than that? What greater vested interest could there be than God's interest in the world, making sure that it bowed to his will, and did everything that he wished? How is it possible to oppose God in any way?

We have the paradoxical answer to questions such as these in this passage. Luke, as he describes the apostles praying together, shows that even the crucifixion of Jesus was evidence of the power of God. Herod and Pilate could not resist God's will, even when they crucified the Lord's anointed, Jesus Christ.

How strange! Again it is in complete contrast to the way that the world thinks. The world thinks power is maintained by force, constraint and oppression. God maintains his power by sacrifice. Against a willing sacrifice nothing can prevail. The power of God is the power of love, of self-giving, rather than of force and majesty.

TO PONDER *The Church is often in danger of lapsing into a sub-Christian understanding of power. For instance, it has sometimes identified it with the oratory of powerful preaching. The power to move others to decision can be used for good or ill: in itself it is not necessarily a sign of the Spirit's presence. The power of the Spirit is the power of love and this may be experienced in every human encounter. It is given to those who desire to be totally available for the purposes of God.*

(Bernard Mobbs)

FRIDAY 20 DECEMBER
GIVING – I

READING ACTS 4:32–37
'Joseph, a Levite from Cyprus, whom the apostles called Barnabas (which means Son of Encouragement), sold a field he owned and brought the money and put it at the apostles' feet' (vv. 36,37, NIV).

BARNABAS is introduced to us at this point. Barnabas, the encourager, would later bring Paul (or Saul as he was then called) to the apostles in Jerusalem. After that, it was Barnabas who fetched Saul from Tarsus and initiated his friend into the great missionary activity of the Church.

9:27
11:22

How appropriate it is that Luke introduces Barnabas in a section devoted to giving, a section which runs across the chapter division, from 4:32 to 5:10. Many people gave, but Barnabas was a prime example of what it means to give, sincerely and completely.

1. Barnabas gave his possessions. He sold a field and donated the proceeds to the central fund. We are not told whether this was all the land he owned. That is not important. What was important was that he gave the whole proceeds of the sale, and kept nothing back.
2. Barnabas gave his reputation when he introduced Saul to the apostles. He risked his standing in the community, putting it at the disposal of the Church.
3. Barnabas gave his position of leadership. He sacrificed it willingly when he realised that Paul had a special calling and special qualities of leadership. The change is described in a subtle manner by Luke. He simply changes the order in which he mentions the two men. 'Barnabas and Saul' or 'Barnabas and Paul' becomes, almost unnoticed, 'Paul and Barnabas'.

11:26; 12:25;
13:2
13:42,46;
14:1,14

Giving involves risk, risking reputation as well as resources. TO PONDER

SATURDAY 21 DECEMBER
GIVING – II

READING ACTS 5:1–11
'A man named Ananias, together with his wife Sapphira, also sold a piece of property. With his wife's full knowledge he kept back part of the money for himself' (vv. 1,2, NIV).

ANANIAS AND SAPPHIRA also gave. Perhaps they gave more, in money terms, than Barnabas. But they deceived the apostles. Claiming to have given the whole price of the land, they actually kept some back. Perhaps their total gift, even after they had siphoned some off for themselves, was greater than Barnabas's gift. We simply don't know.

What we do know is that Ananias and Sapphira were free to do whatever they pleased with their resources. No-one was forced to contribute. And even after the land had been sold, all they had to do was to say 'This is *part* of the proceeds' and all would have been well.

v. 4

Recently, I read an interesting comment on giving one's skills in the service of Christ. J. M. Neale, a prolific hymn writer, wrote in the preface to one of his collections of hymns 'Any compiler of a future hymn book is perfectly at liberty to make use of anything contained in this little book. And I am glad to have the opportunity of saying how strongly I feel that a hymn, whether original or translated, ought, the moment it be published, to become the common property of Christendom, the author retaining no private right in it whatever. I suppose that no one ever sent forth a hymn without some faint hope that he might be casting his two mites into the rich treasury of the Church's hymnody . . . but having so cast it in, is not claiming a vested interest in it something like 'keeping back part of the price of the land?'

Those words were written a long time ago, but how they should be pondered by many in these days of copyright!

TO PONDER   *Is all my skill at the disposal of God, or am I keeping anything back which should be part of the rich treasury of the Church?*

SUNDAY 22 DECEMBER
BODY LANGUAGE

READING LUKE 1:26–38
'"I am the Lord's servant," Mary answered. "May it be to me as you have said"' (v. 38, NIV).

DURING THE PAST FEW YEARS the study of body language has become increasingly important. What we say with our bodies, by gesture and attitude, reinforces or denies the very words we speak. In the verses leading up to today's reading we meet an elderly priest called Zechariah, a religious man who had spent his life serving God. He was a professional in the best sense of the word. Verse six of chapter one tells us about his character, and that of his wife. But despite that, he really did shake his head in disbelief when the vision came. Whilst he worked for God, his body language told the real story.

A young woman named Mary, who was not so much at home in theological matters and the innermost regulations of Jewish religious ceremony, had quite a different response to God's vision and plans. Her response is an example to us all – immediate obedience. Her body language was a reinforcement of her spiritual obedience.

Our Lord, by his coming to earth, gave us all the most perfect example of obedience – revealed through body language. It was not just a matter of gesture and attitude, but of complete commitment of his body, soul and spirit. It is beautifully described in Philippians 2:5–8.

PRAYER SUBJECT: *For perfect obedience, in body and spirit.*

PRAYER: *Our Father in heaven, we praise your name for all the saints who not only said they loved you, but showed it by a bodily obedience to your will. We think about those who took your name to others and became martyrs. Help me not to say 'yes' to you with my words, whilst saying 'no' with my body. Amen, in the name of the Prince of Peace, Jesus our Saviour.*

MONDAY 23 DECEMBER
PROMISES, PROMISES!

READING LUKE 1:67–79
'But when the time had fully come, God sent his Son, born of a woman . . . that we might receive the full rights of sons' (Galatians 4:4,5, NIV).

ALL OF US, at some time or another, have borne the disappointment of broken promises. Our scepticism towards those who never, or seldom keep their word, is seen when – in reply to empty pledges – we whisper inwardly 'Promises, promises . . . !' At times it must have seemed as though God had not kept faith with the Jewish people to send his Messiah. As they read from God's word, did they inwardly mutter, 'Promises, promises . . . !' How do you keep faith alive in promises which seem to be false? It is timing which is all-important.

God's words are never without power and his promises are always kept. The evidence of this is most clearly to be seen in his sending of Jesus. The reaction of Zechariah following the birth of his son, John the Baptist, which we have read today, only reinforces this belief. God has yet to fail to keep a promise.

During Advent our faith receives an enormous encouragement because we are reminded again that God kept his word. Our Christmas carols are full of this sentiment. We sing heartily and with praise such words as

> *Hark the glad sound! The Saviour comes,*
> *The Saviour promised long.*
> *Let every heart prepare a throne,*
> *And every voice a song.*
> *(Philip Doddridge, SASB 81, HFTC 193)*

2 Cor 1:20

The evidence of our own lives is that God is still keeping his word to us through the presence and work of Jesus in our hearts. All his promises are 'yes' in Christ and they really are promises!

TO PONDER *Let us praise God for his faithfulness in keeping his word and for his perfect timing.*

TUESDAY 24 DECEMBER
YONDER SHINES THE INFANT LIGHT

READING MATTHEW 2:1–12
'When they say the star, they were overjoyed' (v. 10, NIV).

IN SOME PARTS of the Netherlands it is becoming fashionable to string a set of Christmas lights on a tree in the front garden. Usually they are displayed so that passers-by have the pleasure of the decorations. However, it is also becoming the case for people to decorate the tree so that the lights can be seen only from inside the house; by those sitting in the cosy front room. Their tree lights are for personal use only. But then such Christmas tree lights cannot make a home any warmer or give light to the heart. It really only shows how differently the world makes merry at 'Xmas' and how Jesus' disciples celebrate the coming of the true light, the Light of, and for, the World.

The Christian knows that his is a festival for the whole of mankind to share and enjoy. All of us who followed his star, found where he lay and worshipped him, have been filled with joy: his star guided us to himself. Because he lives in us, and his life increases in us, we must reflect his light to those who don't know him yet. As light bringers we must never behave so that his star shines only inwards, into our comfortable pews and religious institutions. His light, his star in us, must be facing the street so that others still walking in darkness will be led to him, worship him and also be filled to overflowing with joy.

Let us share a prayer together, used by millions of Christians throughout the world at this time of the year

> *As with gladness men of old*
> *Did the guiding star behold,*
> *As with joy they hailed its light,*
> *Leading onward, beaming bright,*
> *So, most gracious Lord, may we*
> *Ever more be led to thee.*
> *(William Chatterton Dix, SASB 76, HFTC 99)*

A VERSE

CHRISTMAS DAY
THE WONDROUS GIFT IS GIVEN!

READING LUKE 2:1–20
'The time came for the baby to be born, and she gave birth to her firstborn, a son' (vv. 6b,7a, NIV).

AN UNKNOWN Hong Kong poet wrote that God did not send technical assistance to our world, neither a group of experts and advisers under Gabriel's leadership; he didn't send food or the angels' second-hand clothing, nor did he provide extended loans. Instead he preferred to come himself, born in a stable, hungry in the desert and naked on a cross. Through sharing with us he became our bread, and suffering with us he became our joy.

Today we are faced with an eternal mystery which on the one hand silences us because of its magnificance and yet causes us to sing with the angels 'Glory to God in the highest'. But however our soul responds to God's initiative in sending his Son, his coming has to be accepted and experienced as a gift, a wondrous gift, a gift through which 'God imparts to human hearts the blessings of his heaven.' *(SASB 86 v. 3)*

But how are we to receive that gift? What is necessary in order to have Christ in our hearts? This same Christmas carol reminds us that 'No ear may hear his coming; but in this world of sin, where meek souls will receive him, still the dear Christ enters in.' *(SASB 86 v. 3)*

We receive God's wondrous gift, Jesus our Lord, into our hearts through repentance; with a humble heart we ask God to forgive us our sin, promise to follow him and his teachings, and ask him to take over full control of our lives. The gift is free – but it will cost us our life as we now know it.

A VERSE

O may we keep and ponder in our mind
God's wondrous love in saving lost mankind!
Trace we the Babe, who hath retrieved our loss,
From his poor manger to his bitter cross;
Tread in his steps, assisted by his grace,
Till man's first heavenly state again takes place.
(John Byrom, SASB 78, HFTC 78)

THURSDAY 26 DECEMBER
THE REWARD OF THE FAITHFUL

READING LUKE 2:21–35
'My eyes have seen your salvation' (v. 30, NIV).

ALL THAT ADVENT meant and still means is personified in Simeon's life. Despite the spiritual darkness around him, Simeon kept his faith fixed on God who had made promises regarding mankind's salvation. Despite everything happening around him in religious and political life; despite the occupation of his land by the world's greatest power, Rome; Simeon kept his hope in God alive.

Following the Spirit's leadings, he was obedient to the end. His life was one long advent – hoping, waiting, watching for God's promised salvation. Nothing distracted him from living in expectation that God would come and save. Simeon is an example to us all of how we should be living as children of God, privileged enough to be already experiencing, in some measure, 'the blessings of his heaven.' We are living in a second advent period – hoping, waiting and watching for that second coming when Jesus shall return as the conquering Christ who will establish his kingdom finally, and perfectly.

We do well to study Simeon and adopt his religious lifestyle if we want to live like Christ. Our spirits have to be turned to God's Spirit; we mustn't lose heart however dark things may be; we have to become accustomed to looking for God at work in everyday people and events. Especially we ought to be looking for God in those who do not necessarily observe the same religious traditions as we do. Who knows just when Jesus will appear again? We have to be ready, or we shall not see his salvation when he returns. We have to be looking for God.

> *Saints before the altar bending,*
> *Watching long in hope and fear,*
> *Suddenly the Lord, descending,*
> *In his temple shall appear.*
> *Come and worship,*
> *Worship Christ, the new-born King.*
> *(James Montgomery, SASB 75, HFTC 76)*

A VERSE

FRIDAY 27 DECEMBER
DOING A FINE JOB

READING ACTS 5:12–16
'No-one else dared join them, even though they were highly regarded by the people' (v. 13, NIV).

THE SALVATION ARMY is a strange organisation. Being a salvationist is looked upon by many people as odd. It's something you learn to live with, but it's always there. Often, however, a person will overcome embarrassment at meeting a salvationist by saying, 'You people do a wonderful work' or something similar.

It is, of course, nice to be greeted in such a way, and we are eternally grateful to salvationists who have indeed done a wonderful work through the years, providing spiritual and material help in many different situations. However, for every hundred who greet you thus, and for every thousand who are willing to contribute financially, there is probably only one who will come alongside and help the work forward. People admire what others do, but find it difficult to involve themselves in it.

It was like that in the early Church. Many admired the early Christians' love for each other, their sharing, their giving, and their commitment to preaching the gospel. But relatively few dared to join. The thousands who joined were paralleled by many, many thousands who didn't. Many felt afraid – understandably so when we think of how the authorities persecuted the Church. But they also felt uncomfortable. Faced with those who are different, we tend to shy away rather than come together. We may see differences, instead of the common bond of humanity which unites us. We may bring our sick to be healed. We may put others into contact with those who can help – but ourselves?

TO PONDER *The Christian path is one of commitment. It cannot be followed merely by admiring what Christians do, nor even by bringing others to Christ. It can only be followed by bringing ourselves.*

SATURDAY 28 DECEMBER
GOING BACK

READING ACTS 5:17–26
'"Look! The men you put in jail are standing in the temple courts teaching the people"' (v. 25, NIV).

JAIL BREAKS are news. When prisoners escape the media have a field day. They question how it happened, demand greater security, perhaps try to interview relatives and friends. The more spectacular the escape, the more newspapers it sells, and the greater TV coverage it gets. What would today's media have done about the escape of the apostles? It is not hard to imagine.

A banner headline highlighting the angelic rescue, then concentration on the real business, the audacity of these people in going straight back to the temple to preach. The fear of the authorities would be highlighted. Rumours would be started of an attempted coup. The stability of society would be called into question and the apostles would have a hard job convincing people they were not bent on toppling the government of the day.

The apostles' action, not only returning to the scene of the crime, but re-committing the crime for which they had been imprisoned, was an audacious one. Even in those days, without media attention to magnify their action out of all proportion, they created a stir. Their influence was great enough to terrify the authorities. Officials could not imagine the apostles' motives were anything but political. They could not envisage a motivation which went beyond self-interest.

Returning to the scene of the 'crime' was, for the apostles, an act of costly self-sacrifice. How easily they could have fled to safety. How easily they could have turned the escape to their own interest. But no, they went straight back to the place of conflict, contending for the gospel.

Do I welcome the opportunities God offers by returning to the conflict, or by seeking refuge from it? TO PONDER

SUNDAY 29 DECEMBER
OBEYING GOD

READING ACTS 5:27–32
'"We must obey God rather than men! . . . We are witnesses of these things, and so is the Holy Spirit, whom God has given to those who obey him"' (vv. 29b,32, NIV).

IN PRINCIPLE, Christians are obedient to secular authorities. Jesus himself told us to give the state its due (Mark 12:13–17). We have loyalties to employers, to business associates, to localised authorities of many kinds which, by and large, we are happy to recognise, and which for the most part generate little conflict with regard to our Christian principles.

However, occasions of conflict can arise. A Christian worked for a company selling swimming pools; on the face of it a morally neutral activity. Swimming is a beneficial pastime, and where resources are available, why should swimming pools not be built? But increasingly he was being asked to deal with private customers. At first, in the affluent Britain of the eighties, there seemed little harm. If someone could afford a swimming pool, why not? Then he was asked to sell abroad, which he did, until he was asked to go to Portugal, and then to Ethiopia. In Portugal the contrast between his wealthy clients and the shanty towns strung along the highway hit home. In Ethiopia the obscenity of providing a luxury pool in an area of life-threatening water shortage made him rethink his career. He could no longer obey his employers. Resignation followed, and the search for a new job.

He made the break. He had listened to the voice of God, the prompting of the Spirit. The decision was still not easy. The point where we finally say 'We must obey God rather than men' is not always as clear-cut as between the apostles and the temple authorities. Only with the Spirit's guidance can we resolve such conflicts. Sometimes it will mean making the break. Sometimes it will mean great tension trying to witness in a situation which is less than ideal.

PRAYER SUBJECT: *Praising God for the gift of his Spirit.*

PRAYER: *Thank you, Lord, for the gift of your Holy Spirit. Thank you for the eternal mystery of his continuing presence with us.*

MONDAY 30 DECEMBER
GAMALIEL

READING ACTS 5:33–39
'In the present case I advise you: Leave these men alone! Let them go! For if their purpose or activity is of human origin, it will fail. But if it is from God, you will not be able to stop these men; you will only find yourselves fighting against God' (vv. 38,39, NIV).

THE MINOR CHARACTERS of the Acts of the Apostles are a fascinating collection. Christian or not, each has a special contribution to make. Gamaliel is one of the most interesting. His simple statement to leave the apostles alone and see how things work out has reverberated through the centuries and become a byword for wisdom. If it is from God, it will prosper, if not it will fail. What a dangerous doctrine!

History is littered with figures who, left alone, succeeded and only came to failure when they were massively opposed. It is at our peril that we forget the opening words of today's highlighted portion 'in the present case'. Gamaliel's advice is not something we can apply universally. He never intended it so. Under the Spirit's guidance, surely, he was led to advocate a policy of live and let live *in this particular instance*.

As a general principle it may be more true to say, along with Edmund Burke, that 'the only thing necessary for evil to triumph is for good men to do nothing'. Only in specific cases can we say that, when left alone evil will perish. Ultimately, yes, but that is a matter for the next world, not this.

As with so many Old Testament figures before him, and even as Peter himself on the day of Pentecost, Gamaliel spoke words whose truth was greater than he realised. In this instance the only thing to do was to let the apostles alone, for God was with them.

Acts 2:17
WoL 7 Dec

We cannot shirk the responsibility to oppose evil by quoting Gamaliel! TO PONDER

TUESDAY 31 DECEMBER
PERSUASION

READING ACTS 5:40–42
'His speech persuaded them. They called the apostles in and had them flogged. Then they ordered them not to speak in the name of Jesus and let them go . . . [The apostles] never stopped teaching and proclaiming the good news that Jesus is the Christ' (vv. 40,42b, NIV).

WE REMAIN WITH GAMALIEL for this final comment of 1991. It is the close of a chapter. Official, legal attempts to stop the growth of the Church were halted by the intervention of Gamaliel. A minority of one, he persuaded the rest of his legal colleagues to let the apostles go. But his words had no effect on the rabble's spontaneous, unofficial persecution which would shortly lead to the stoning of Stephen. Presumably encouraged by those in authority who had failed to silence the apostles through the legal process, the rabble continued the fight by every means possible.

7:57ff.

However, the apostles could not be persuaded to silence, even by flogging. Right was on their side. They were prepared to meet the tide of opposition and struggle against it. Their new life in Christ gave them strength to pursue his aims with singleness of mind and a steadfast purpose.

Today, Christians face a different, more subtle, tide of opposition. It carries us along, gently persuading us 'It's all right to walk in the same direction as the crowd'. It coaxes us into complacency, inviting us to believe that democracy, the opinion of the majority, the rule of the people, will solve our problems. It sets standards by the lowest common denominator of economic forces, instead of by the highest common factor of dependence upon Christ our Saviour.

Let the evidence of our God-dependent life be that we never stop teaching and proclaiming the good news that Jesus is the Christ.

TO PONDER *The only fish that swims with the stream is a dead fish.*
(Malcolm Muggeridge*)

*Malcolm Muggeridge died the day before this comment was written.